50 Tables:
Innovations in Design and Materials

M

M.

50 TABLES

Innovations in Design and Materials

Mel Byars

Introduction by
Sylvain Dubuisson

Research by
Cinzia Anguissola d'Altoé
Brice d'Antras

Drawings by
Marvin Klein

A RotoVision Book

PRO DESIGN SERIES

RotoVision

Published by RotoVision SA
Rue du Bugnon, 7
CH–1299 Crans-Près-Céligny
Switzerland

RotoVision SA
Sales & Production Office
Sheridan House
112/116A Western Road
Hove, East Sussex BN3 IDD, England
Tel: +44 1273 7272 68
Fax: +44 1273 7272 69

Distributed to the trade in the United States
Watson-Guptill Publications
1515 Broadway
New York, NY 10036
U.S.A.

ISBN 2–88046–311–4

This book was written, designed, and
produced by Mel Byars.

Printed in Singapore
Production and separation
by ProVision Pte. Ltd., Singapore
Tel: +65 334 7720
Fax: +65 334 7721

PRO DESIGN SERIES

50 Chairs: Innovations in Design and Materials
by Mel Byars with an Introduction by Alexander von Vegesack

50 Tables: Innovations in Design and Materials
by Mel Byars with an Introduction by Sylvain Dubuisson

50 Lights: Innovations in Design and Materials
by Mel Byars with an Introduction by Paola Antonelli

50 Products: Innovations in Design and Materials
by Mel Byars with an Introduction by David Revere McFadden

Contents

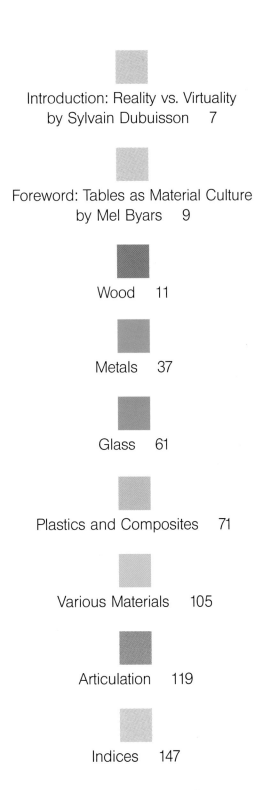

Introduction:
Reality vs. Virtuality

The table, as well as the chair, has become an irreducible part of the history of furniture production and likewise of our daily lives. In order to have some insight into the role and form of the table, let's contrast it to the chair which, besides being a highly functional object, has manifestations corollary to those of its users—human beings—and even to society as a whole. The less-demonstrative table plays a secondary role to the chair but is no less significant.

When we look at tables and chairs as archetypes (or ideal forms), their individual differences are obvious. The centuries-long continuity of their forms has made it possible for us to isolate the ideas we have developed for each one—a relatively readable schema engraved in our thoughts and variously incarnated in the production of different models through the ages.

Essentially the archetype which the chair embodies is a fundamental contradiction: the front legs reach only to seat level while the rear ones rise higher to become the back rest. This disparity gives rise to an essential ambiguity and, in another sense, the impurity of all chairs to which a great many designers have responded with varying levels of mastery and virtuosity. Attempting to diminish the problem, increase efficiency, and lessen the ambiguity, Modernists have attempted to resolve the contradiction by making chairs with stool-like characteristics: the seat and the back form a single unit, held aloft by a configuration of legs or a base of some kind. That chairs are an essential index through which an interpretation of society may be conjured is precisely based on this confrontation with their ambiguity—an archetypal ambiguity which is a manifestation of life itself, in all its complexity.

Contrarily, tables present an altogether different order. The archetype of a chair is obvious and simple: a surface is supported by a leg or legs or other device to raise it from the ground. There is no ambiguity here. The history of the table, past and present, may be read as infinite variations on a very simple theme to which all tables more or less refer.

Variations of tables have primarily concerned the technology called upon to make tables and devise their forms. The entire history of classical styles was bound to an unchanging tradition in skills, mainly in woodworking. The technology employed to produce a table for a king was the same as that used by, for example, the Shakers.

Exponents of the Modern Movement—motivated by extreme, utopian leanings—have tended to identify with the archetype, as attested by the work of Mies van der Rohe and the group Archizoom. However, the Modern Movement is today as much before us as behind us.

In the wake of the healthy confusion encouraged by Postmodernism, few people today are attempting to bring an element of clear-sightedness to bear on new, emerging products. Mel Byars is one of the few. Offering great originality and an exemplary concern for methodology, in this book he lays bare and dissects 50 versions of a wide range of tables. We may count on his vision to bring us pleasure through his elucidation.

Keep in mind that since the recent advent of the microprocessor, tables and chairs no longer have quite the same meaning as before. Electronics have irreversibly invaded our daily lives with increasingly efficient and ever-smaller objects. While virtuality has imperceptibly evolved into reality, tables and chairs still present their same, immutable characteristics: heights of 46cm for chairs and 75cm for tables continue to be unalterably linked to their use and to the body sizes and shapes of the users.

We might even think of the present as the age of confrontation between objects which originated as archetypes (like board games) and objects which originated in dematerialized forms (like computer games). To the extent that dematerialization follows technology's vertiginous progress, archetypes are beginning to look more and more archaic. And, as the real is erased and we are swept into the virtual, our need for the presence of the archaic is becoming more urgent.

A desire to re-establish a balance between the two has created the need for a tangible validation of our existence in the world we live in. And the more technology and communication contribute to making virtuality a worldwide phenomenon, the better we are able to appreciate the reality, for example, in the technical inventiveness of the tables chosen by Mel Byars. Could it be that the creation of variety is a reaction to the prevailing proliferation of dematerialization?

Sylvain Dubuisson
Paris

Foreword:
Tables as Material Culture

Because chairs and tables are the most important pieces of furniture in any environment, *50 Chairs* was the obvious choice for the first volume in the Pro-Design series and, hence, *50 Tables*, the second. But it was with some trepidation that I chose to include a book on tables, regardless of their ubiquity.

My initial reticence was based on the unfounded judgment that tables in general, especially new tables, would not be interesting, indeed particularly boring. Therefore, why do a book that would be dull? Yet, ignoring my initial concerns and proceeding with the intension of preparing a book on tables, I discovered that I had been naïve, probably just ignorant. Much to my delight I found a wide range of tables that had been created by imaginative designers who, when put to the task, whether self- or manufacturer-assigned, had conjured a number of fascinating examples, including those that express the surreal if not impractical, those that voice serious and highly functional concerns, those that address green matters, and those that feature ingeniously manipulated materials.

A distinct effort was made to include examples by both male and female designers from all six continents whose work transcends the merely utilitarian use of new and traditional materials, resulting in the remarkable and the intelligent.

There are five basic kinds of tables: for dining, for work, for playing games, for handy convenience (like the coffee table and small side table), and for use while standing (like the buffet/hunt table and the console). They serve as evidence that the study of design must always focus on sociological, anthropological, political, and financial concerns rather than primarily aesthetic ones. The tables in this book that fold or breakdown speak of the scarcity of environmental space; ones in inexpensive materials concern frugality; ones featuring multiple functions illustrate the single service of one utilitarian object for many; and ones that appear to be simple may be essentially quite intricate while others that appear to be simple are indeed quite simple. And all of them have sprung forth, whether facilitatively or arduously, from the constantly probing minds of designers, not always serious nor solely playful.

The choices here are my personal ones, limited by the images and documentation which I and my assistants were able to collect from the generous manufacturers and designers who accepted our invitation to participate. There were certain other tables we wanted to include but were unable to get the necessary materials to fulfill adequately the promise of the book: how new tables are made and what thinking goes into their realization. But, alas, we were able to satisfy the quota of 50 examples, including some intriguing ones suggested by my assistants and hitherto unknown to me.

This book purposefully does not contain a bibliography, designer biographies, or lengthy prose. The commentary, except this essay, is intensionally brief and has been laid out in a manner to make it quickly comprehensible, but hopefully the images perform most of the work of telling the story of each object.

I am schizophrenic about the books in the Pro-Design series, confessing that I am uneasy on the one hand and prideful on the other that the books emphasize the clever and artful exploitation of new and traditional materials, methodologies, and technologies rather than aesthetics. My discomfort stems from the backlash against the adulation of science generally and of technology specifically. The indictment alleges that the unharnessed pursuit of technological development for profit is incompatible with a respect for the planet. Thus, in part, the cries are that an ecological catastrophe has already happened. The reproach includes the romantic assertion that, while focusing on science, the enjoyment of nature is lessened.

As a response and not a pardon, I share an apocryphal story about Hermann Helmholtz, the 19th-century German physicist and anatomist. He was traveling in the mountains of Switzerland with some friends when a great storm arose. Helmholtz, being of a scientific disposition, assiduously began to scribble observational notes. His friends asked him if this rationalization of one of nature's great dramatic moments did not distract from its beauty, to which he rejoined that, on the contrary, the phenomenon became all the more dramatic and moving.

But, even so, the Pro-Design series does not concern the value of the Earth-helping or Earth-harming production and processes employed in the creation of the objects in the volumes but rather is offered as a report, and not a thorough one, on a narrow slice of our material culture as expressed during the last decade or so. But be warned; some of the materials used to make furniture, furnishings, and products, especially right now, may indeed be both harmful to the makers and to the users. In the production of fine art, sculptor Niki de Saint-Phalle, for example, can attest to the the life-threatening effects of certain substances that give off toxic gases. The emission occurs not only when the substances are being manufacturered but also

Foreword

up to four and five years after. A single case in point: particle board, which many of us have considered harmless, gives off highly toxic fumes.

There are no assertions here to suggest that anyone needs to purchase, own, or use the tables discussed. Probably no one does. And the book is not intended as an advertising medium for the products; nepotism was punctiliously avoided, although I and my assistants are friendly with some of the designers and the representatives of the manufacturers. I thought hard and long before including the "Corinthia" table system by the husband of one of my assistants. She merely presented the table to me along with many others without any special comment or urging. I could have omitted it without a reprisal. Neither she nor the designer knew of its inclusion until after publication.

The final selection of tables, numbered from one to 50, is arbitrarily grouped according to materials or some other distinguishing characteristics. While there is a rainbow of examples, the group is not necessarily representative of the state of the table today, only somewhat exemplary and then not widely so.

If the examples serve to amuse, enlighten, delight, provoke, or infuriate you, then we have done our job well. But be assured that bore you they will not.

Mel Byars
New York City

Wood

Table

Designer: Axel Kufus (German, b. 1958)
Manufacturer: the designer
Date of design: 1987

The most notable feature of this table is the elimination of blocks for reinforcement which would normally be added to the underside of a sparsely built, thin-framed table such as this one. The simplicity of its construction is complemented by the simplicity of the design itself: four leg-sides and a top. To decrease waste, the large pieces of wood removed to form the legs are used by the designer to make his "Stöck" chairs.

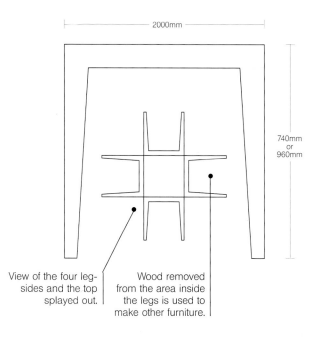

View of the four leg-sides and the top splayed out.

Wood removed from the area inside the legs is used to make other furniture.

Plan view of the corners.

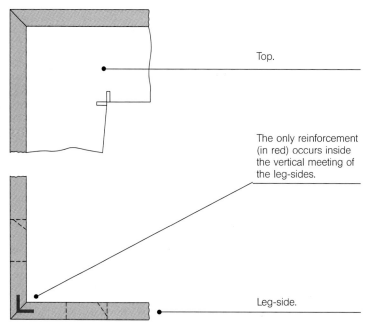

Top.

The only reinforcement (in red) occurs inside the vertical meeting of the leg-sides.

Leg-side.

Table

The five film-coated plywood sections (four
leg-sides and the top) are cut using templates.
After gluing, the edges are given a fine edge.

The raked angle of the thick plywood, the one-piece
leg-side, and the special glue all contribute to the
elimination of underside block reinforcement.

The mitered (45°) 12mm-
or 15mm-thick plywood
(shown here at the top
of the leg-side) is being
coated with glue by the
designer-maker.

"Herr Zock" table

Designer: André Haarscheidt
(Swiss, b. 1966)
Manufacturer: the designer
Date of design: 1995

This table is exemplary of standard
type-furniture, extreme in its use
of plain materials whose natural
features are revealed. The raw
edges of the wood are left to view;
the details of the construction are
exposed.

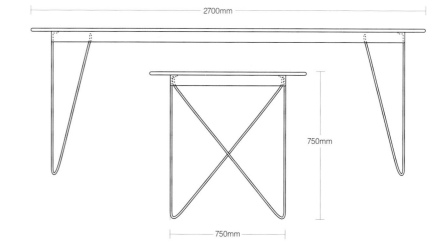

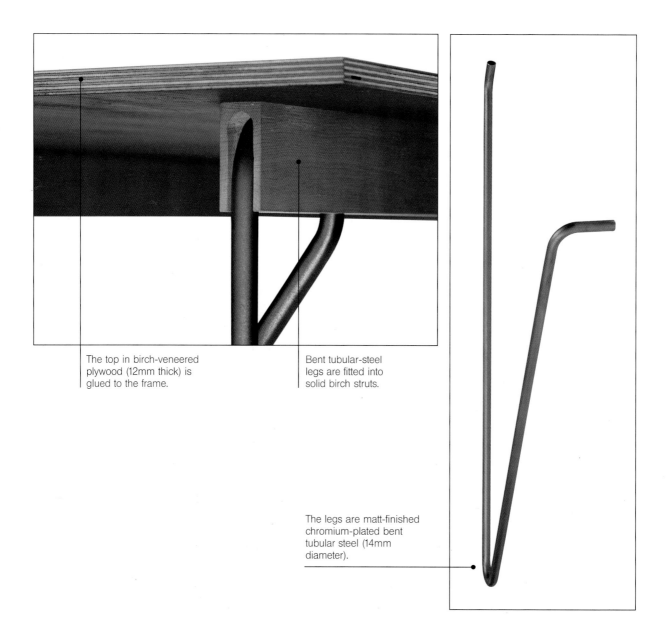

The top in birch-veneered
plywood (12mm thick) is
glued to the frame.

Bent tubular-steel
legs are fitted into
solid birch struts.

The legs are matt-finished
chromium-plated bent
tubular steel (14mm
diameter).

"Chromosome" side table

Designer: Essaime (né Stéphane Millet,
French, b. 1949)
Manufacturer: Quart de Poil', Paris, France
Date of design: 1996

In limited production, this table was
commissioned to mark the centenary of
the French magazine, *Art et Décoration*.
Deceptively complicated and pivoting
along two different axes, the legs
must be positioned correctly (held
to the top by magnets) for the table
to function properly.

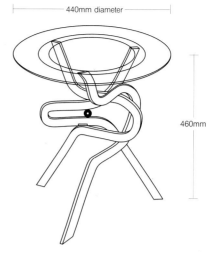

The legs are folded by rotating them around
two different axes. The base and glass top
can be displayed on a wall like a bas-relief
sculpture or hung on a wall merely to store
it out of the way. Weighing 4Kg, the size
when folded is 450mm x 450mm x 30mm.

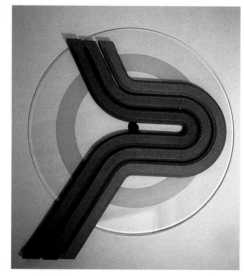

Three steel disks are UV. (ultraviolet) glued to
the etched circle on the Sécurit tempered-
glass top, indicating the position of the legs;
otherwise the legs will not function properly.

Iron magnets (3Kg pull each) are attached to
the tops of the three legs to adhere them to
the steel disks glued under the glass top.

Two iron axles and bolts are inserted
through two areas of each of the three legs.

Three legs of MDF (medium-density
fiber) compressed wood are stained
and varnished.

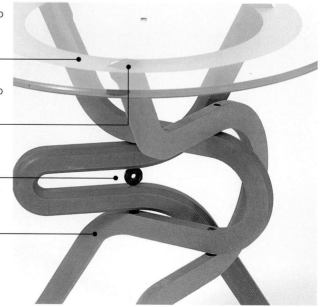

"Oh! Marie-Laure" table

Designer: Christian Ghion (French, b. 1958)
and Patrick Nadeau (French, b. 1955)
Manufacturer: G.N. Éditions, Paris, France
Date of design: 1996

A new approach to the manipulation of
plywood, the sheets (from which the four
sections of this table are cut) are bent before
the cutting is performed. The designers,
employing the kind of technological
innovation made possible by the computer,
have successfully incorporated a pleasing,
flowing aesthetic flare into an object that
might have been mundane in the hands
of others.

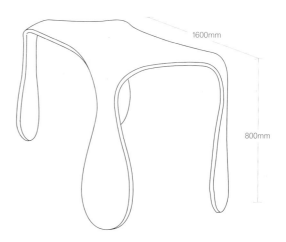

Plywood (27mm thick) is steam
bent prior to its being cut into
four pieces (or two matching
shapes) by digital-numeric
instructions from a computer.

The four sections of the table (two
separate shapes) are glued together.

(Only three of the four sections are
shown here, awaiting the fourth to be
cut from the steam curved section
shown above.)

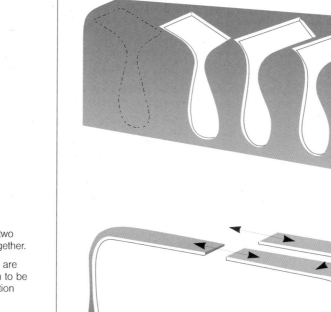

"Max" table

Designer: Ruud Ekstrand (Swedish, b. 1943)
Manufacturer: Inredningsform AB, Malmö, Sweden
Date of design: 1992

A relatively simple, traditional approach, this table combines the predictable simplicity and material (wood) one has come to expect from Scandinavian craftspeople. The top is an unattached component available in one of three different materials. The object has no secrets; all the joints and hardware are left naked.

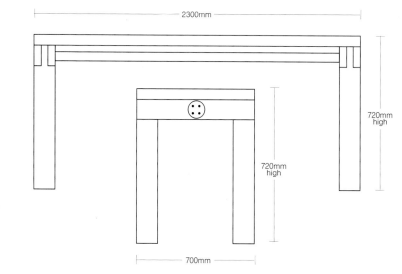

Available in a range of sizes and heights, measurements of only the basic model (MAX HB 701) are given here.

Exploded view of the stainless-steel hardware and stretcher.

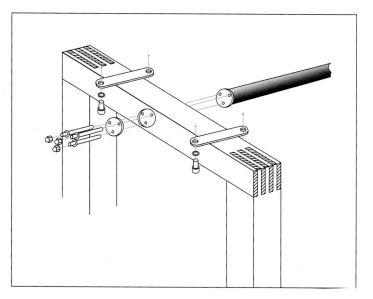

Tops available in solid beech (30mm thick), gray-brown lime-stone (30mm thick), or clear glass with a polished edge.

Solid beech.

Stainless-steel hardware.

Exposed mortise work.

Stainless-steel stretcher.

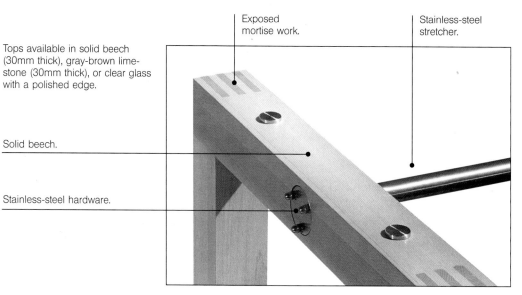

"Arquà" table

Designer: Carlo Bimbi (Italian, b. 1944)
and Paolo Romoli (Italian, b. 1941)
Manufacturer: Diber, Tavernelle di
Serrungarina (PS), Italy
Date of design: 1995

A simple solution was employed for a
vexing problem. This ambitious table
features tubing for the legs that is inserted
into round holes in a wooden block. The
tubes are held in place by a cylindrical
tensioning technique that creates a sturdy
structure to be assembled by the user.

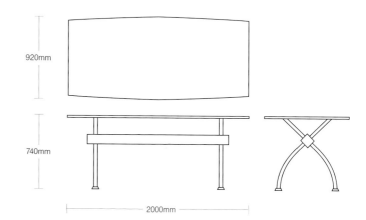

920mm

740mm

2000mm

The glass top is 15mm thick with beaked
edges or with 45°-angle edges. The
glides (at the ends of the legs) are turned
aluminum, hand polished and painted
with acrylic varnish.

Solvent stained, acrylic painted,
or natural stained/waxed solid
cherrywood.

Electrowelded aluminum (45mm
diameter), polished and coated
with acrylic varnish.

A blocking expansion system holds
the aluminum legs in place by a
hex screw that is tensioned by a
hex screwdriver provided to the
user who assembles the table
himself.

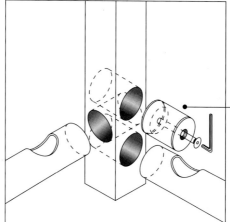

Expanding cylinder that
holds the aluminum legs
firm, when inserted into
the wooden girder.

7

"Legs" center table

Designer: Laura Agnoletto (Italian,
b. 1963) and Marzio Rusconi Clerici (Italian,
b. 1960)
Manufacturer: Adedei Tre S.r.l.,
Milano, Italy
Date of design: 1990

With a complexity that far exceeds its
function, this fascinating table's design
elements are based on zoomorphic
elements: the spider, the crab, and the
tortoise. These sections are held by a
tension structure that employs cable that
can be tightened. The glass top, shown
rectangular here, can be almost any
shape or size. Surprisingly, the legs are
of wood, not metal.

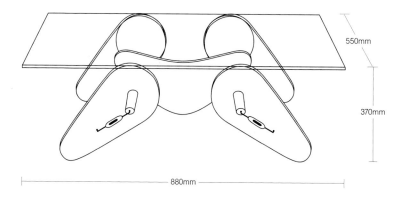

550mm

370mm

880mm

Hand-painted birch-veneered
plywood (10mm thick).

Aluminum
shaft cone.

A tension cable holds
together the different
sections (a rubber piece
intended for a boat draft
and a steel tie-beam).

Threaded steel rod (with
tension cable attached to
the end) is inserted into the
aluminum shaft cone.

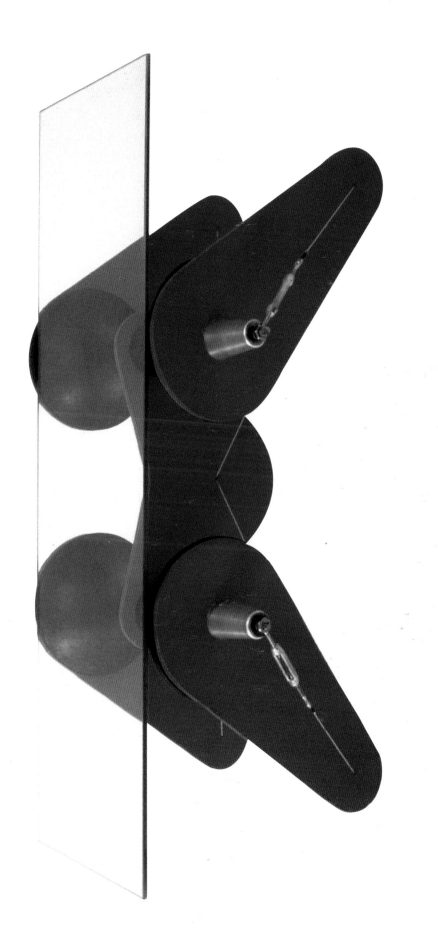

8

"TV Stage" unit

Designer: Katsushi Nagumo (Japanese, b. 1956)
Manufacturer: Tokyo Mitoya Co. Ltd., Tokyo, Japan, and Project Candy-Milano, Milano, Italy
Date of design: 1994

Cabinets that house remote-controlled high-fidelity equipment and audio-visual components require that closed doors be "transparent" enough to permit the beams of UV (ultraviolet) beam to pass through. Most cabinets have incorporated doors made of smoked translucent glass or plastic, although the equipment remains somewhat visible. The unit here offers an interesting design solution to the problem: solid wood-composition doors with slit piercing.

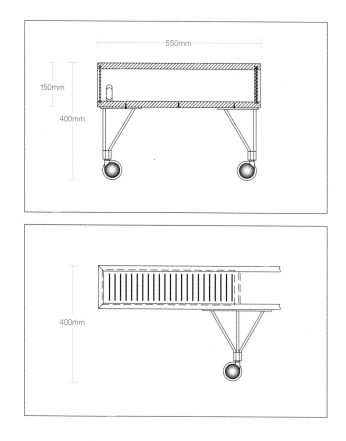

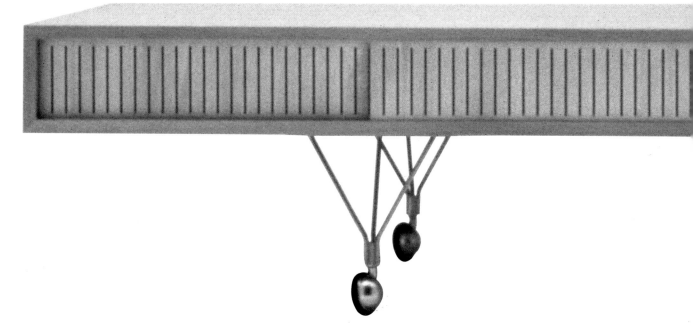

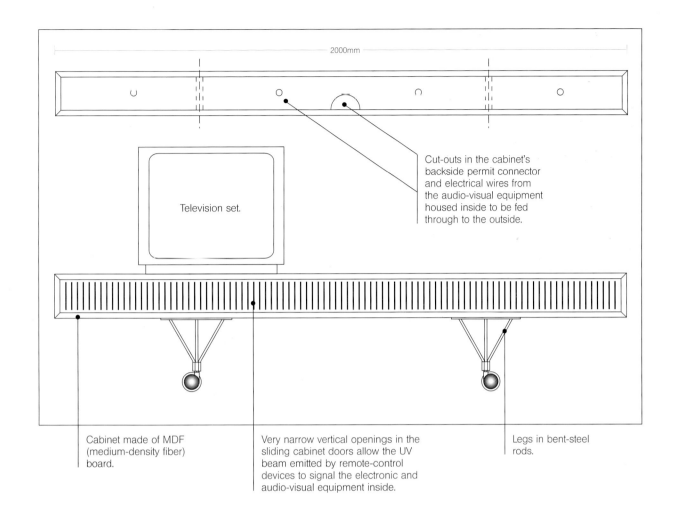

2000mm

Television set.

Cut-outs in the cabinet's backside permit connector and electrical wires from the audio-visual equipment housed inside to be fed through to the outside.

Cabinet made of MDF (medium-density fiber) board.

Very narrow vertical openings in the sliding cabinet doors allow the UV beam emitted by remote-control devices to signal the electronic and audio-visual equipment inside.

Legs in bent-steel rods.

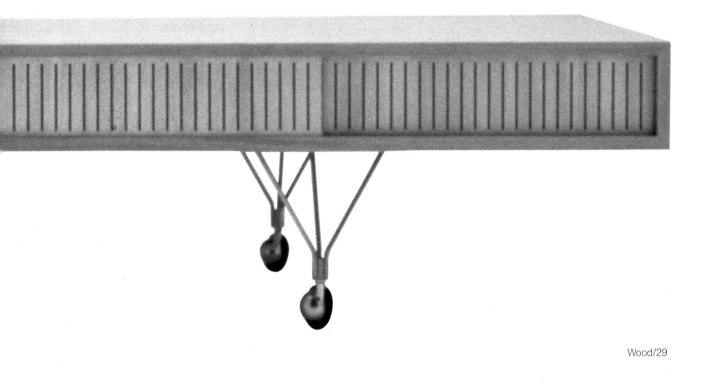

"Ply" table

Designer: Jasper Morrison (British, b. 1959)
Manufacturer: Vitra AG, Weil am Rhein,
Germany
Date of design: 1990

Even though mass produced, this table is
made with great care by craftspeople in a
large factory using advanced machinery
technology. Designed by a British person
for a German firm, the table is very simple
and made with a relatively small number of
pieces. But, unlike the table (pages 12–15)
by Axel Kufus which is made with thicker
wood, this table requires underside blocking for reinforcement.

1500mm

750mm

720mm

Wood/31

9

"Ply" table

Sequential images illustrate the production sequence.

1500mm x 3000mm x 15mm birch-veneer plywood.

Full plywood sheets being cut into sections.

Leg templates.

A CNC (computer) program guides the templates.

Stacks of leg parts await attachment.

Leg corners are glued together before being attached to the top.

The production sequence continues

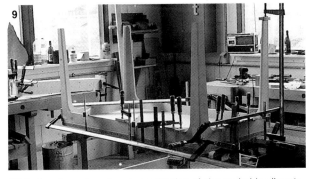

A craftsperson carefully attaches the legs to the top.

Leg corners are held in place by clamps.

While the glue sets, a baroque collection of clamps holds all parts.

A completed table is sanded and cleaned.

A table, elevated from the floor, is spray-painted on all sides, including beneath. The paint is a clear DD solution known as Pur varnish, with additives that provide a high resistance to UV (ultraviolet) light.

"Spanoto" table

Designer: Jakob Gebert (German,
b. 1965)
Manufacturer: Nels Holger Moormann, Aschau im
Chiemgau, Germany
Date of design: 1996

The very definition of type furniture, this unadorned
table can be shipped and stored flat; the top is
used as the container. No special tools are
required for its quick assembly which is realized
with the use of a wooden paddle that separates
the tops of the legs before they are slid into side
tracks on the bottom side of the top. However, this
table does appear to be somewhat unstable.

1600mm/1900mm/2200mm

860mm

740mm

"Spanoto" table

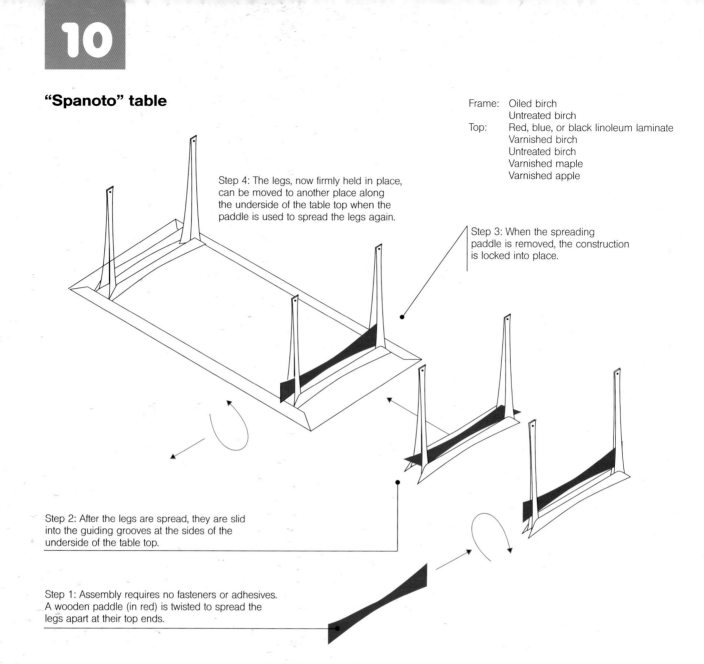

Frame: Oiled birch
        Untreated birch
Top: Red, blue, or black linoleum laminate
        Varnished birch
        Untreated birch
        Varnished maple
        Varnished apple

Step 4: The legs, now firmly held in place, can be moved to another place along the underside of the table top when the paddle is used to spread the legs again.

Step 3: When the spreading paddle is removed, the construction is locked into place.

Step 2: After the legs are spread, they are slid into the guiding grooves at the sides of the underside of the table top.

Step 1: Assembly requires no fasteners or adhesives. A wooden paddle (in red) is twisted to spread the legs apart at their top ends.

Metals

"Wounded Knee" adjustable table

Designer: Jonas Lindvall
(Swedish, b. 1963)
Manufacturer: David design ab,
Malmö, Sweden
Date of design: 1992

This table employs simple materials—
wood and metal. A screw element in
the stem is adjustable by the sitter's
knee, permitting the table top to be
turned for height adjustment, much
like some office chair bases.

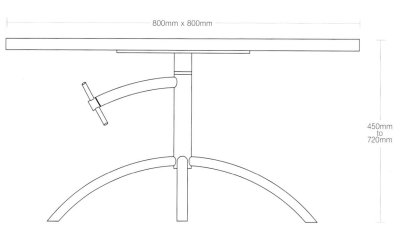

800mm x 800mm

450mm
to
720mm

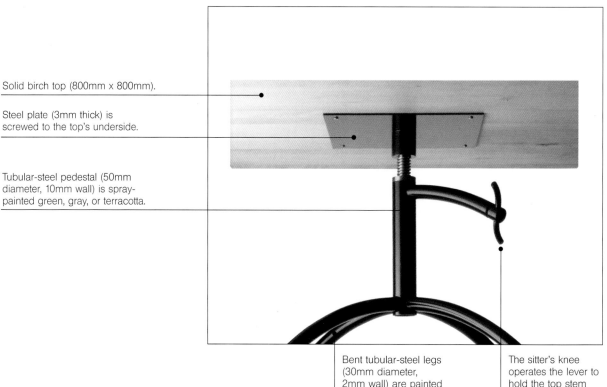

Solid birch top (800mm x 800mm).

Steel plate (3mm thick) is
screwed to the top's underside.

Tubular-steel pedestal (50mm
diameter, 10mm wall) is spray-
painted green, gray, or terracotta.

Bent tubular-steel legs
(30mm diameter,
2mm wall) are painted
to match the pedestal.

The sitter's knee
operates the lever to
hold the top stem
tightly, holding the
height firm.

"Manthis" adjustable table

Designer: Alberto Liévore (Argentine, b. 1948)
Manufacturer: Perobell, Sabadell, Spain
Date of design: 1990

This table is highly functional, intelligently mechanical, and well conceived while featuring a curious angular form, which announces its insect namesake. The pitched stem, that adjusts vertically, holds the top-tray in a horizontal position.

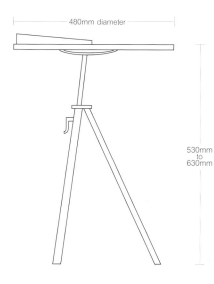

480mm diameter

530mm to 630mm

Top tray is available in stainless steel or a chromed-black finish like the base, or in cherrywood-stained ash with a metal base.

The top is raised and lowered by the stem inserted into the tubular back leg.

Release lever to adjust the tray height.

The three-leg frame is soldered together.

A developmental drawing reveals the designer's interest in creating a vertically adjusting table.

"High Func" table legs

Designer: Olof Kolte (Swedish, b. 1963)
Manufacturer: David design ab, Malmö,
Sweden.
Date of design: 1991

Produced by an aluminum foundry, the
legs are steel-shot blasted after casting.
Available in two heights, the legs are to
be attached by the end user to a table
top in almost any kind of wood. While
not particularly inexpensive, the use of
recycled aluminum is admirable.

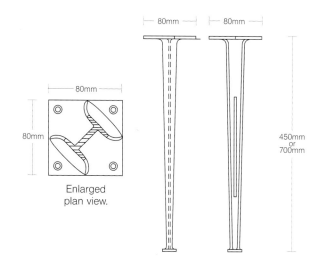

Enlarged
plan view.

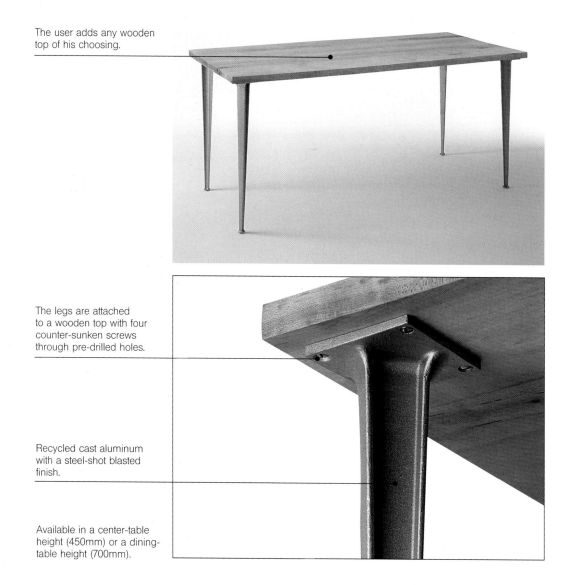

The user adds any wooden
top of his choosing.

The legs are attached
to a wooden top with four
counter-sunken screws
through pre-drilled holes.

Recycled cast aluminum
with a steel-shot blasted
finish.

Available in a center-table
height (450mm) or a dining-
table height (700mm).

"Dumbo" side table

Designer: Piero Gaeta (Italian, b. 1961)
Manufacturer: Steel, divisione della Molteni
& Molteni S.p.A., Giussano (MI), Italy
Date of design: 1994

Part of the manufacturer's Domestic Zoo
group of furniture, this table is essentially a
fatuous object—a *folie* with high technological standards, a fine finish, and great
attention paid to detail. In featuring an
animal form, the design rejects the total
abstraction found in most tables and may
be favorably compared to the robust animal
forms found in 19th-century Black Forest
furniture. Evidently popular, there were
800 examples of this table produced.

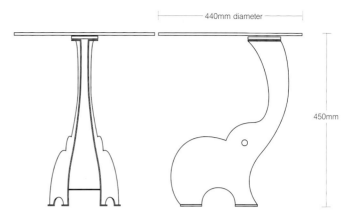

Clear glass top (440mm diameter,
5mm thick) with polished edges.

Steel disk is screwed to the base
and epoxy glued to the glass.

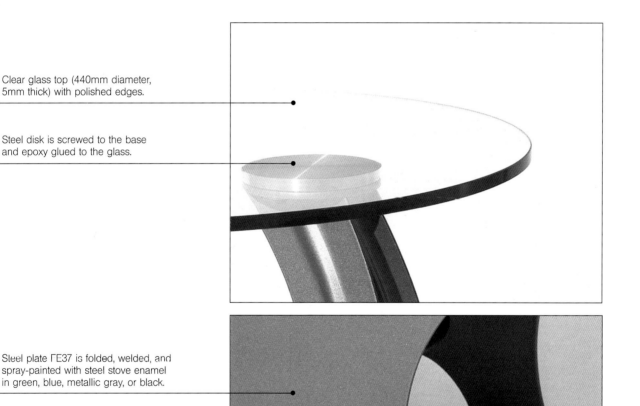

Steel plate ГE37 is folded, welded, and
spray-painted with steel stove enamel
in green, blue, metallic gray, or black.

"Nomos" table system

Designer: Norman Foster (British, b. 1935)
Manufacturer: Tecno S.p.A., Milano, Italy
Date of design: 1986

A highly flexible system, a wide range of table configurations are made possible by the large inventory of available parts and pieces. For example, tops can be had in rectangular or round shapes and flat or, for drafting use, tiltable. The design, while appropriate for domestic use, provides the kind of flexibility today's office environment demands, including the addition of lighting fixtures, storage units, and other components. Arguably, the concept is supposed to be simple enough to allow easy assembly and manufacture worldwide.

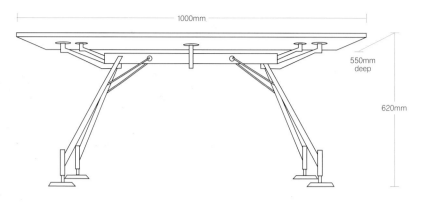

Of the seven sizes available including those with round tops, only the no. T1016 is shown above and right.

Foot design.

The parts, steel fused onto aluminum, are finished in polished chromium plating or powder painted in metal gray or shiny black colors.

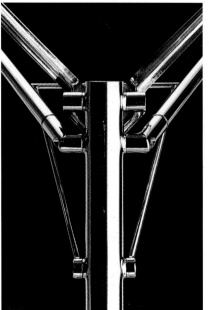

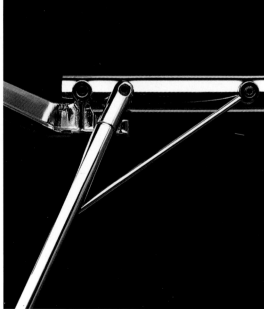

15

"Nomos" table system

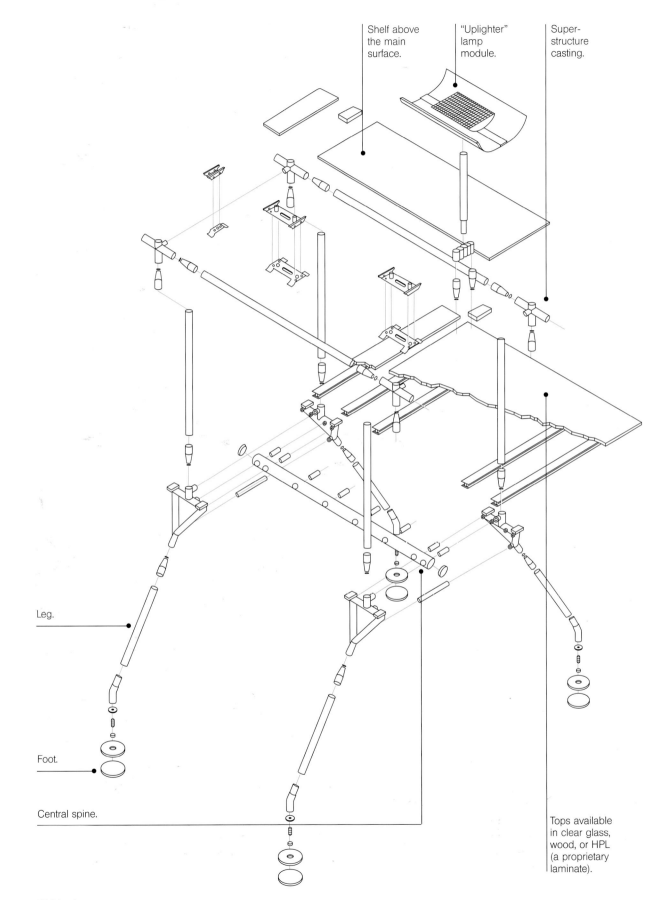

Shelf above the main surface.

"Uplighter" lamp module.

Super-structure casting.

Leg.

Foot.

Central spine.

Tops available in clear glass, wood, or HPL (a proprietary laminate).

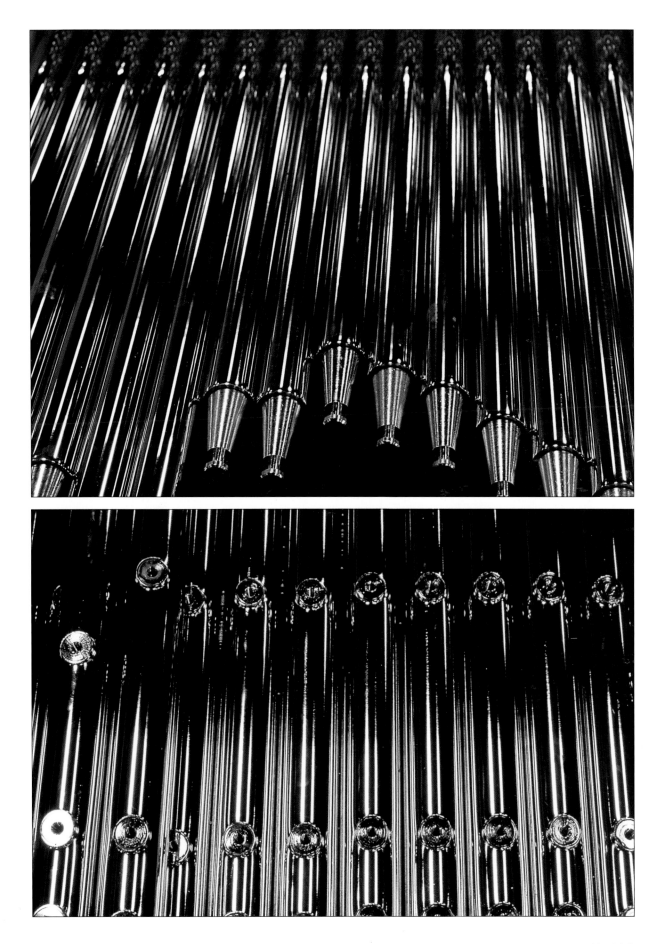

"Chincheta" center table

Designer: Sergi Devesa i Bajet
(Spanish, b. 1961) and Oscar Devesa i Bajet
(Spanish, b. 1963)
Manufacturer: Disform S.A., Barcelona, Spain
Date of design: 1987

The essential design principle of this table
is based on very simple geometry. A circle
of sheet aluminum is cut with only a straight
line in three places equally spaced along the
perimeter and bent downward.

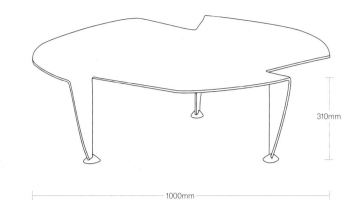

310mm

1000mm

Available in gray or black
epoxy spray-painted
aluminum.

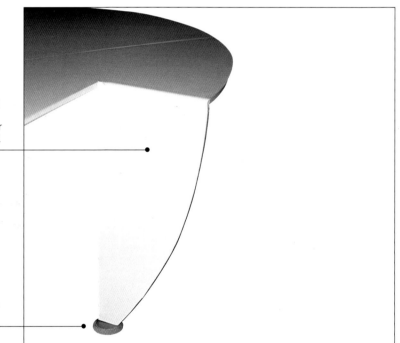

The leg section is created
by one straight line sawn
into the 1000mm-diameter
top and bent down at 90°.

Leg tips in cast aluminum
L-2560-60.

Small maquettes were
made prior to production.

"Corinthia" table system

Designer: Luca Scacchetti (Italian, b. 1952)
Manufacturer: Poltrona Frau, Tolentino (MC), Italy
Date of design: 1995–96

Intended for executive office and conference room use, numerous configurations are made possible through the use of various parts, sections, and fittings—all part of this ambitious system. In the suite, there are matching cabinets, bookcases, shelf units, a low center table, and lighting (none shown here). Based on Postmodern principles, the aesthetic reflects classical forms, thus the abstracted Corinthian capital at the top of the leg.

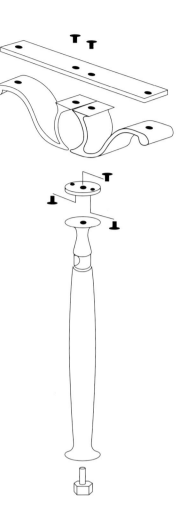

The support system is made of polished extruded aluminum.

A light metal frame is fitted with turned chromium-plated steel columns.

"Corinthia" table system

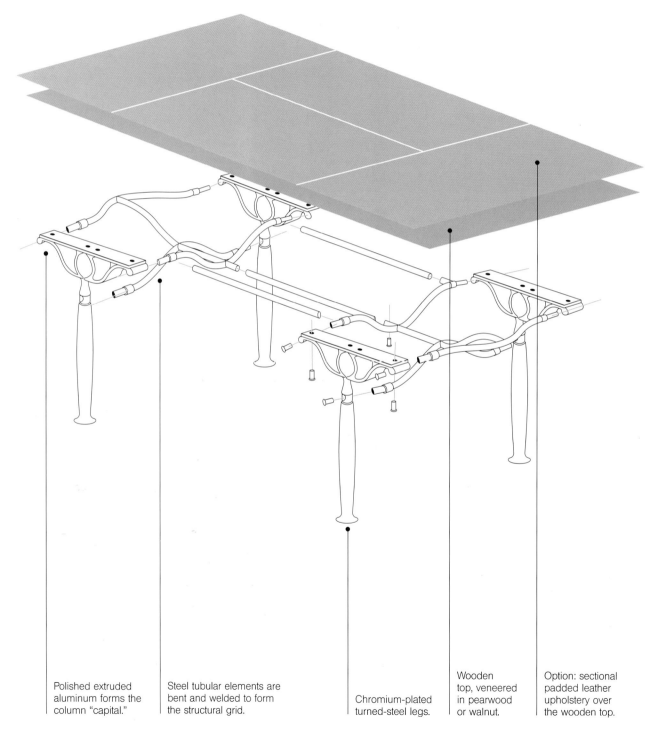

Polished extruded aluminum forms the column "capital."

Steel tubular elements are bent and welded to form the structural grid.

Chromium-plated turned-steel legs.

Wooden top, veneered in pearwood or walnut.

Option: sectional padded leather upholstery over the wooden top.

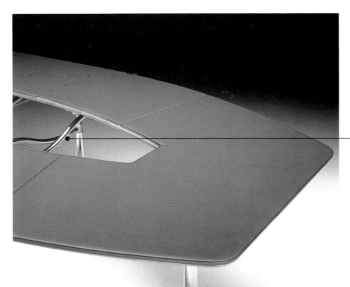

Center areas can be wired for electricity or filled in with clear glass or matching wood.

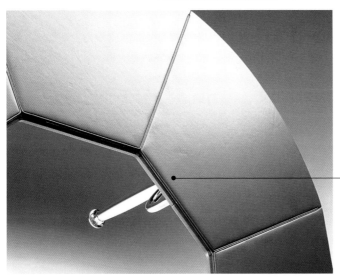

Work surface, in wood with rounded edges, can be upholstered in leather (a product for which the manufacturer has become well known) or can be veneered in pearwood or walnut.

Modularity facilitates a wide range of sizes and configurations.

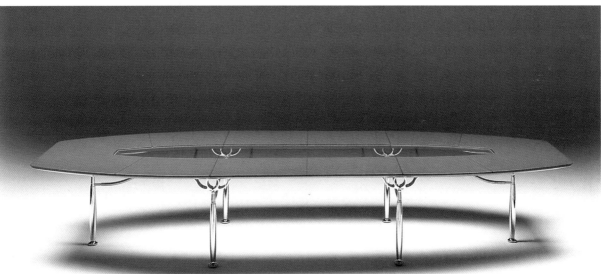

"Less" table system

Designer: Jean Nouvel (French, b. 1945)
Manufacturer: Unifor S.p.A., Turate (CO), Italy
Date of design: 1993

As part of a suite, this table-desk system was designed especially for the Fondation Cartier in Paris, France, before being placed into mass production by the manufacturer. In general, very thin-top tables greatly tend to sink in the center part of the top when even a light-weight object is placed on it. Though very thin, the "Less" top gives the illusion of being much thinner than it really is. A group of four counter-reinforcing triangles, fitted together under the top plane, are longitudinally reinforced by welded-on steel strips. Even though the table top slopes down to a thickness of 40mm at the center beneath the flat surface, the overall thickness of the top appears to be only as thick as its supernarrow edge.

"Less" table system

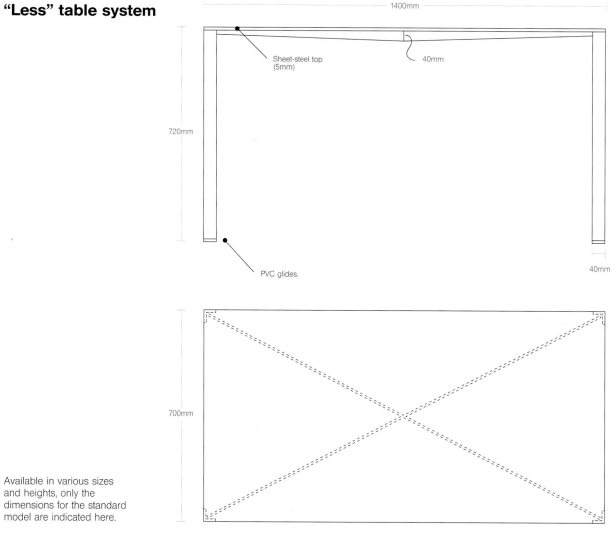

1400mm

Sheet-steel top
(5mm)

40mm

720mm

PVC glides.

40mm

700mm

Available in various sizes
and heights, only the
dimensions for the standard
model are indicated here.

CNC (computerized-numeric control)
eliminates sizing errors, making a
tight fit of the parts possible.

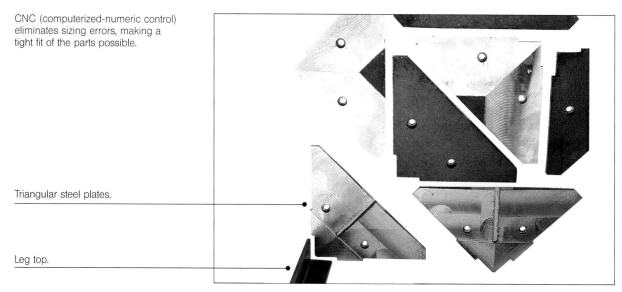

Triangular steel plates.

Leg top.

Triangular steel plates are welded to the leg tops, then glued to the top and bottom sections.

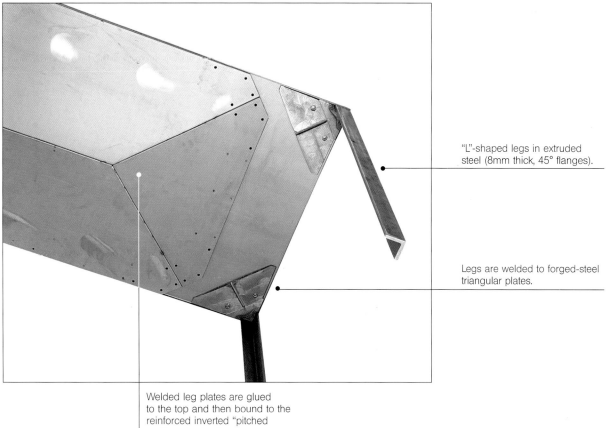

"L"-shaped legs in extruded steel (8mm thick, 45° flanges).

Legs are welded to forged-steel triangular plates.

Welded leg plates are glued to the top and then bound to the reinforced inverted "pitched roof" understructure.

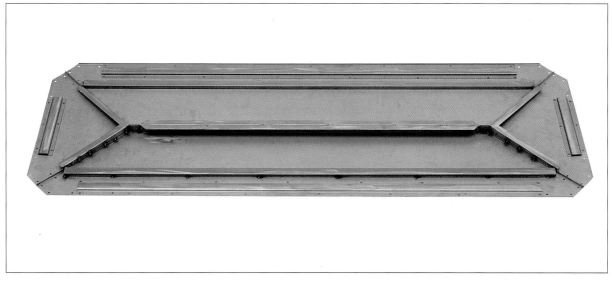

The welded "pitched roof" understructure (above) offers the necessary resistance to prevent the top from sagging under weight.

"Less" table system

A center table version is placed in the interior space of the Fondation Cartier, Paris, for which the system was originally created.

View of the superstructure beneath the sheet-steel flat top. All surfaces are polyurethane painted and then polyacrylic coated.

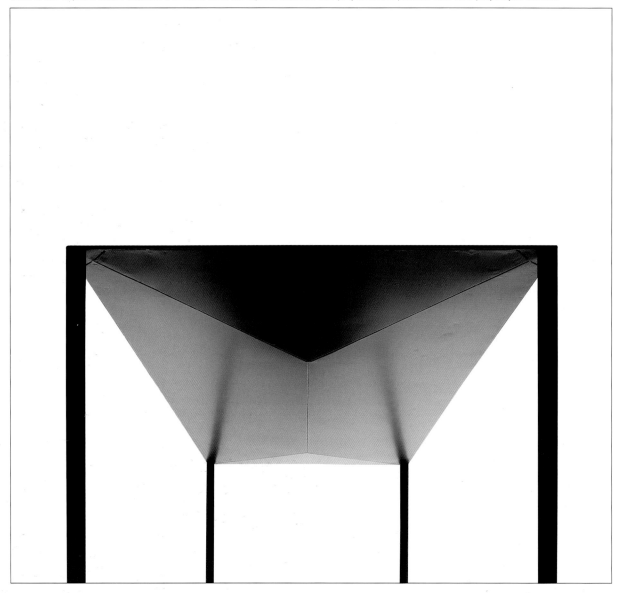

Glass

19

"Fleur" center table

Designer: Vincenzo Lauriola (Italian, 1962–93)
Manufacturer: Porada arredi S.r.l., Cabiate (CO), Italy
Date of design: 1992

A prototype, this table is an exercise which illustrates how to combine engineering-tension principles with pleasing aesthetic values. The high-tech materials include hole-bored plastic and steel disks and epoxy glue used to hold the disks to the underside of the glass top.

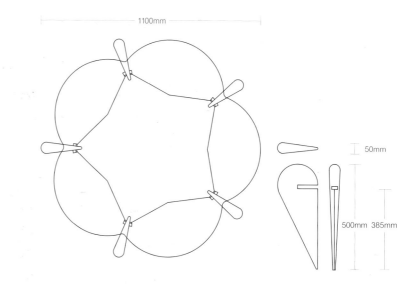

Five stainless-steel disks are epoxy glued to the underside of the glass table (notice the reflection).

Taut steel cable (2mm thick) is fed through the plastic-eye element of the steel disks.

Five legs in cherrywood are rounded on all sides.

The quintafoil-shaped clear glass top (15mm thick) has a polished edge.

Cable is fed through plastic tubes fitted into each leg.

Cable-threaded disks are glued to underside of the clear-glass top.

20

"Table de Verre II"

Designer: Philippe Chaix (French, b. 1949)
and Jean-Paul Morel (French, b. 1949)
Manufacturer: Sté Forma, Paris
Date of design: 1991

The designers of this table—principally
architects—have worked in collaboration
with Woytek Sepiol to develop furniture
which has explored the use of glass and
new materials. This example is made
almost entirely of glass, with the exception
of steel rods running through the legs and
topped by metal disks.

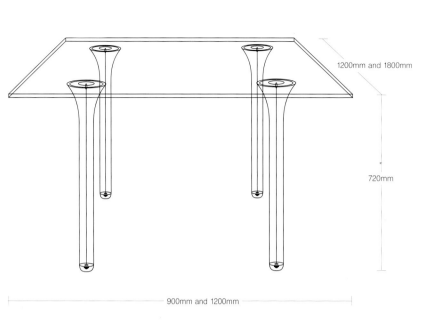

1200mm and 1800mm

720mm

900mm and 1200mm

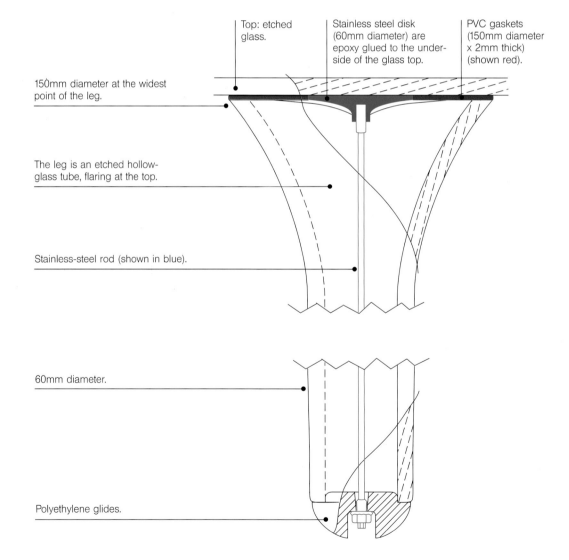

Top: etched glass.

Stainless steel disk (60mm diameter) are epoxy glued to the under-side of the glass top.

PVC gaskets (150mm diameter x 2mm thick) (shown red).

150mm diameter at the widest point of the leg.

The leg is an etched hollow-glass tube, flaring at the top.

Stainless-steel rod (shown in blue).

60mm diameter.

Polyethylene glides.

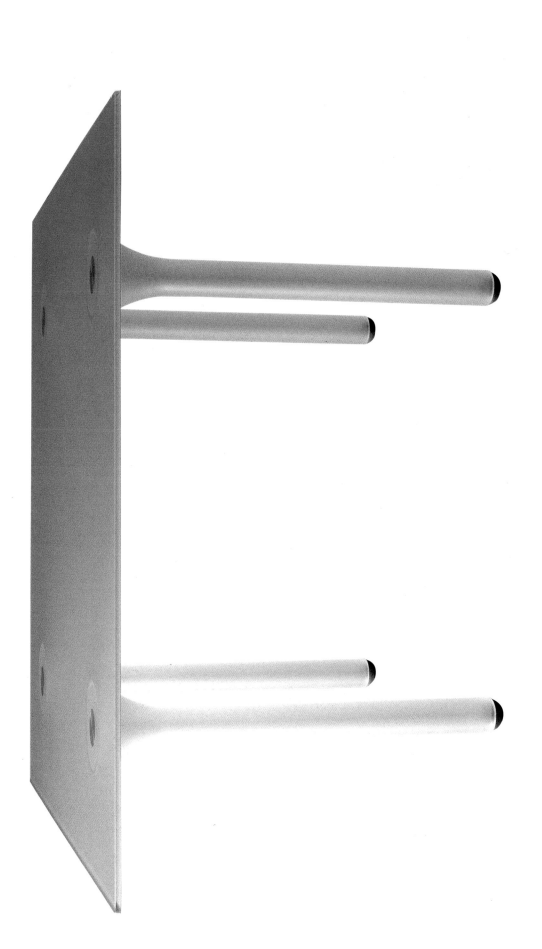

21

"Tala" table

Designer: Chérif (né Chérif Médjeger,
French b. 1962)
Manufacturer: wood version Tenon et Mortaise,
for VIA, Paris, France; glass version Group de
Verriers Associés
Date of design: 1987

This side table was produced in two versions:
one in wood and one in glass. The editions
were 100 examples in wood and three in
glass. The former version is an Old World
statement employing traditional craftsmanship,
while the glass version is an experimentation
in the use of a fragile but efflorescent material.
Both were exercises that married the efforts of
artisans and designer. While not cheap, neither
are the tables inordinately expensive.

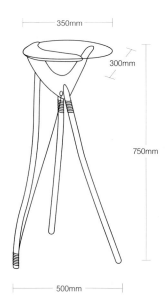

350mm
300mm
750mm
500mm

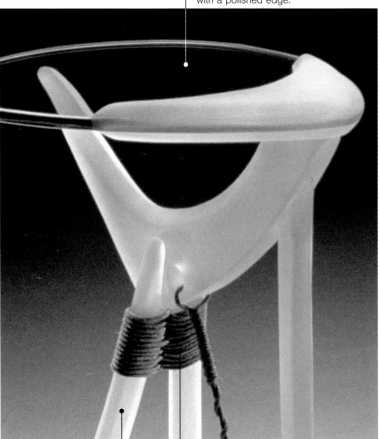

Clear-glass top surface
with a polished edge.

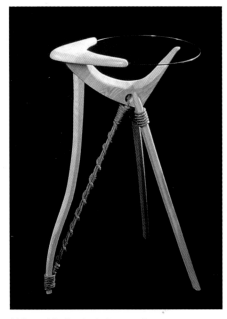

Using a binding technique and rope
material, the ashwood frame was made
by the artisan group, Tenon et Mortaise.

Rope is adhered with an
UV-fixed adhesive.

Acid-etched glass frame and
construction produced by
Group de Verriers Associés
(three glassmakers).

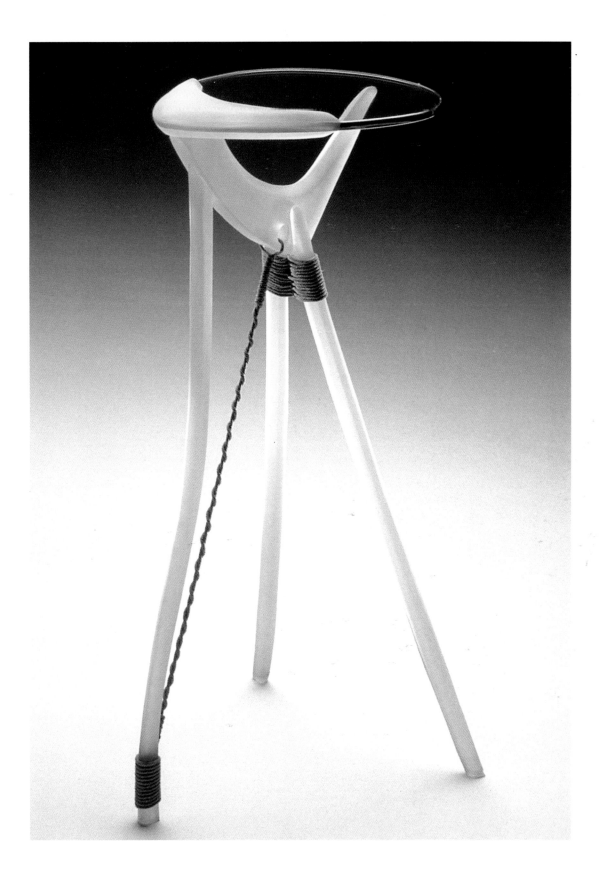

"Ragno" table

Designer: Vittorio Livi (Italian, b. 1944)
Manufacturer: Fiam Italia S.p.A., Tavullia (PS), Italy
Date of design: 1984

Fiam, founded in 1972, has become known for
its daring one-piece glass furniture. This table,
made soft in an oven after being cut from one
piece of flat glass, is notable for its simplicity
and conception, a departure from the manufacturer's other more intricate glass furniture.

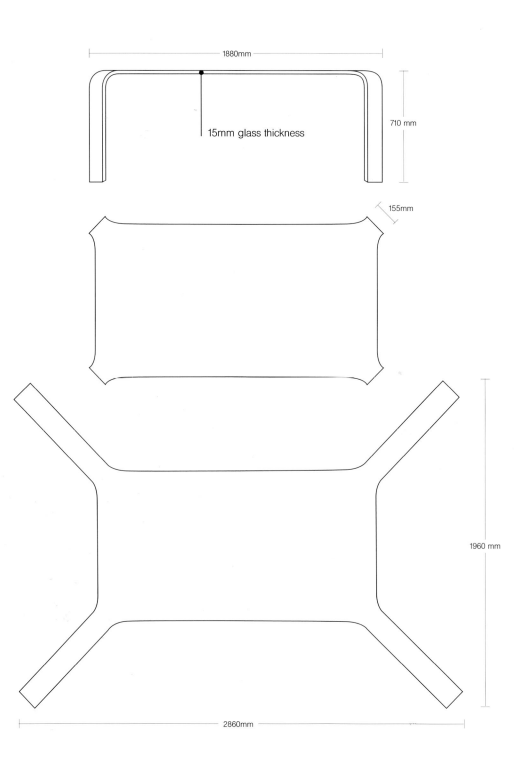

1880mm

710 mm

15mm glass thickness

155mm

1960 mm

2860mm

"Ragno" table

So-called float crystal is warm bent in a tunnel furnace (exterior shown above), using an exclusive process developed by the Fiam Italia firm. One year's technological studies were spent in developing the "Ragno" table. (A different object is being softened in the furnace below, but a similar oven and the same process is employed.)

Plastics and Composites

23

"Hatten" side table

Designer: Ehlen Johansson (Swedish, b. 1958)
Manufacturer: IKEA, Ålmhult, Sweden
Date of design: 1992

Typical of the inexpensive goods for which the manufacturer has become known, this table features a top that doubles as a removable tray. The tray rests on the body drum that serves as a storage area. Assembly is performed by the user. With retail stores worldwide, IKEA sells a great many products; for example, 28,000 copies of this table have been made each year since 1993.

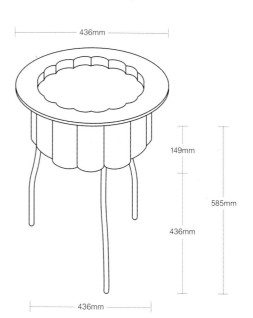

The tray-lid atop and basin below are of a thermoformed acrylic in transparent, blue, and red versions. (Red was replaced by orange later in the production run.)

Aluminum tubing (16mm diameter).

Plastic glides are fitted into the leg ends.

24

Composite table

Designer: Sylvain Dubuisson (French,
b. 1946)
Manufacturer: Moc, Chavignon, France
Date of design: 1987

This very lightweight table is built with
high-tech materials in a design so refined
as to make almost no decorative statement.
Issued in an edition of five, the object with
its superthin top is more of an intellectual
statement than an artistic one, although
its aesthetic values are not insignificant.

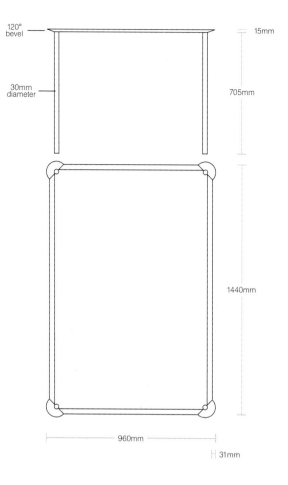

The edges are beveled from below to
make the table appear wafer thin. The
bevel is rectilinear along the sides and
ends and conical at the four corners,
forming a 120° angle.

The constituents are in polyurethane foam
(15mm thick): the outer layer of the top is
a carbon-fiber taffeta pre-impregnated with
epoxy resin 3000 filaments (thickness
4/10), and the intermediate layer is a high-
modulus carbon fiber and a film of mono-
component bond in epoxy.

The seam was necessary due to the
narrow width of the carbon-fiber taffeta.

The tops of the tubular legs (30mm
diameter, in braided carbon fiber for
the first version and stainless steel for
the second) are inserted into short
tube inserts which are attached to
the underside of the table top.

Neoprene glides are attached to the ends of
the legs (not shown).

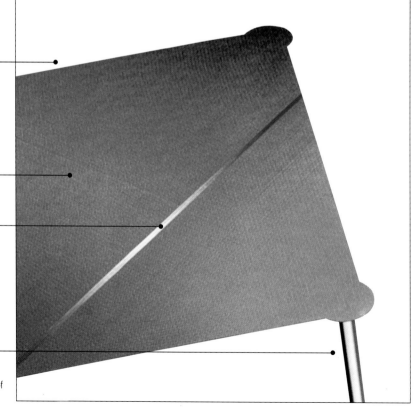

"Plaky" side table

Designer: Christopher Connell (Australian, b. 1955) and Raoul Hogg (New Zealander, b. 1955)
Manufacturer: MAP (Merchants of Australian Products), Victoria, Australia
Date of design: 1993

The top and legs of this table were produced by molding a substance composed of recycled ABS (acrylonitrile-butadiene-styrene) and recycled polycarbonate materials. The table has also begun to be produced with cast resin (facing page).

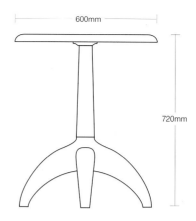

Revealing their first-life colors, the reprocessed polycarbonates and ABS, previously used in other products, are chopped up, re-extruded, granulated, and molded.

The top is bolted to the aluminum pedestal.

The molded leg-base, composed of a recycled, speckled mixture like the top, is bolted to the hollow-core aluminum pedestal.

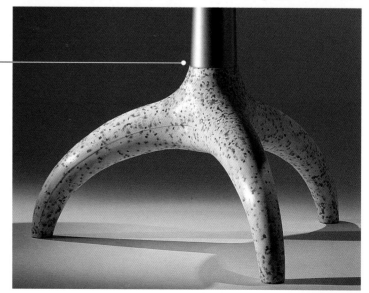

Inflating table

Designers: Fernando Campana (Brazilian, b. 1961) and Humberto Campana (Brazilian, b. 1953)
Manufacturer: Campana Objetos Ltda, São Paulo/SP, Brazil.
Date of design: 1996

With removable legs, the idea of the designers, who are brothers, was to produce a table that was its own package. When the bladder body is deflated it is storable while still attached to the top and bottom dishes. The table, appropriate for use by the side of a chair, is inexpensive, amusing, and surprisingly functional. The final version is made in clear PVC.

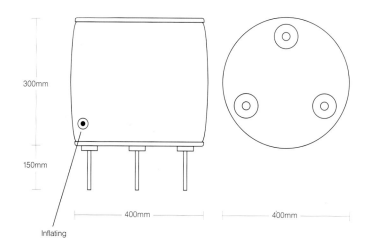

300mm

150mm

Inflating

400mm

400mm

The prototype in yellow PVC (polyvinylchloride) film illustrates the inflatable nature of the object. The legs on the final version are vertical.

All metal is electrostatically spray-painted. The PVC bladder is formed by heat sealing, and the aluminum dishes are contact glued to the PVC.

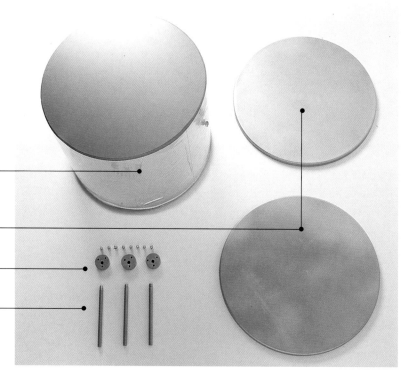

The final version of the table is realized in 0.3mm-thick clear PVC (400mm diameter x 296mm high), supplied by Lidice Brinquedos Ltda, Diadema SP, Brazil.

Two 0.2mm thick aluminum dishes (400mm diameter x 15mm deep).

Leg-socket disks (37mm diameter x 27mm thick) cut from aluminum rods.

Aluminum-rod legs (9mm diameter x 150mm long).

Inflating table

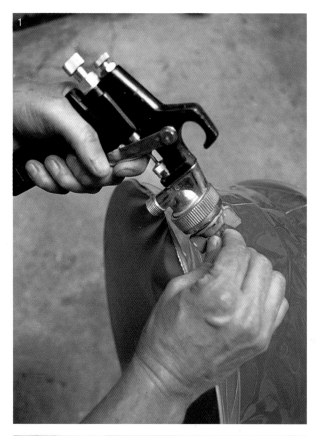

Sequential assembly procedure:

1. An air gun inflates the PVC bladder-body of the table.

2. Contact glue is painted onto the aluminum dishes used for the top and bottom.

3. The top dish is being glued onto the bladder-body.

4. The bottom dish is being glued onto the bladder-body.

5. The legs are screwed into the bottom dishes.

6. The completed, inflated table.

27

"Gello" side table

Designer: Marc Newson (Australian, b. 1963)
Manufacturer: Trois Suisse, Paris, France
Date of design: 1994

An ephemeral, transparent object, this table continues the designer's use of challenging materials to produce intriguing furniture forms. The table, available in one of three colors or clear and packaged flat in a cardboard box, is to be assembled by the end user.

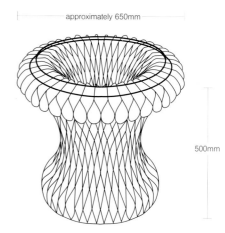

approximately 650mm

500mm

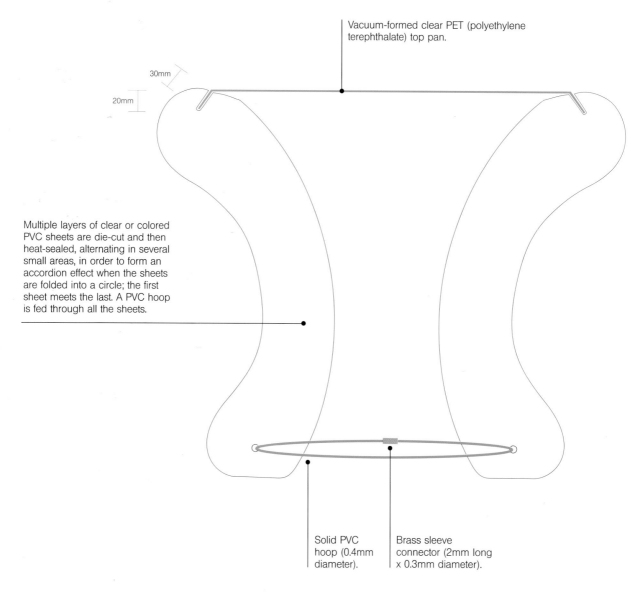

Vacuum-formed clear PET (polyethylene terephthalate) top pan.

30mm

20mm

Multiple layers of clear or colored PVC sheets are die-cut and then heat-sealed, alternating in several small areas, in order to form an accordion effect when the sheets are folded into a circle; the first sheet meets the last. A PVC hoop is fed through all the sheets.

Solid PVC hoop (0.4mm diameter).

Brass sleeve connector (2mm long x 0.3mm diameter).

28

Center table

Designer: Christophe Pillet (French, b. 1959)
Manufacturer: Limited edition for V.I.A., Paris,
for the Carte Blanche award (1993)
Date of design: 1993

Active since 1988 when he designed a
lamp for Memphis, the designer here
explores the use of a heat-formed plastic
material which he combined with metal.
The former, a polycarbonate, produces a
certain frosted translucence, reminiscent
of etched glass.

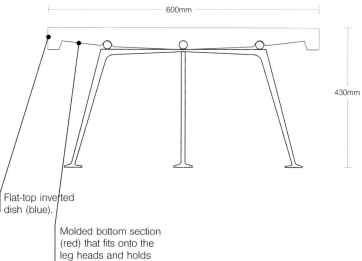

600mm

430mm

Flat-top inverted
dish (blue).

Molded bottom section
(red) that fits onto the
leg heads and holds
the top dish aloft.

The top is formed like a round
box with a flat lid and a sculptured
bottom.

Thermoformed two-part top:
The flat-top inverted dish (above)
forms a hollow box with the
molded bottom (below) that
is held stationary by the
impressed grooves.

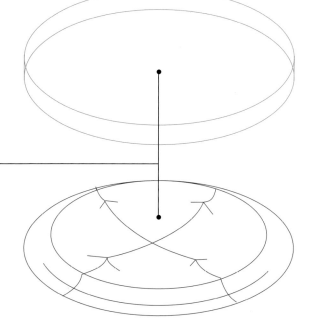

Cast aluminum base.

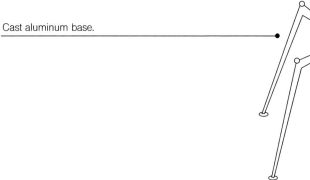

29

"X-Light" table

Designer: Alberto Meda (Italian, b. 1945)
Manufacturer: Alias S.r.l., Grumello del
Monte (BG), Italy
Date of design: 1989

This is an example of the kind of super-
light-weight furniture for which the designer,
who began as an engineer, has become
known. Producing prototypes himself, he
employed machinery necessary to make a
sandwich of glass and carbon fibers in an
epoxy-resin matrix. The external edge is
aluminum. (For a similar leg form, see
René Herbst's 1935 stainless-steel table in
Yvonne Brunhammer, *Le Mobilier 1930–
1960*, Paris: Éditions Massin, 1997, p. 66.)

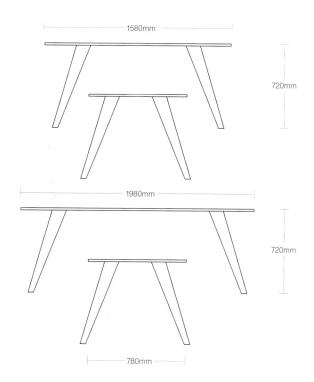

All the components used
in the table's construction.

Aluminum
profile.

Glass-fiber
fabric.

Aluminum
honeycomb.

Carbon-fiber
fabric.

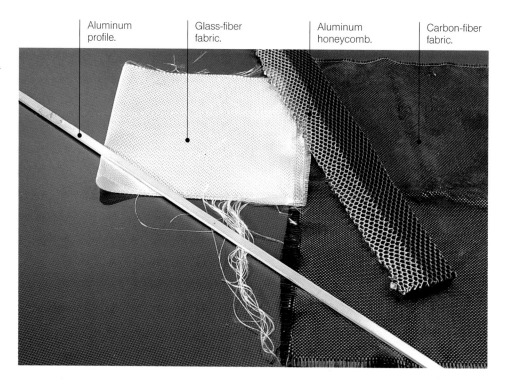

"X-Light" table

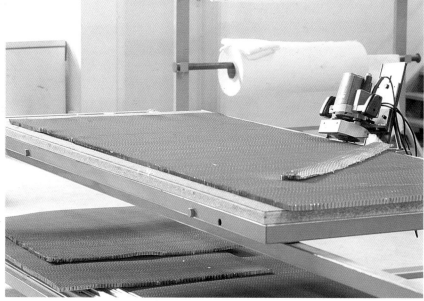

Cutting machine reduces the
thickness of the aluminum
honeycomb near the edge.

Close-up view of the
cutting head.

The external edge of the top is aluminum, and the legs
are made of satin-finished aluminum sheeting.

30

"ANTic" center table

Designer: Marc Harrison (New Zealander,
b. 1970)
Manufacturer: ANTworks, Moorooka,
Australia
Date of design: 1996

The components of this distinctive table that
looks more like a flying saucer are connected by only four screws. Local Australian
wood (for the top) is combined with a resin
(for the superstructure) and steel tubing
(for the legs) to form a relatively simple but
stylish structure produced in a small edition.

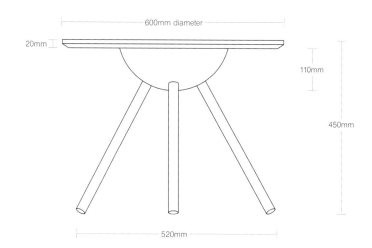

600mm diameter

20mm

110mm

450mm

520mm

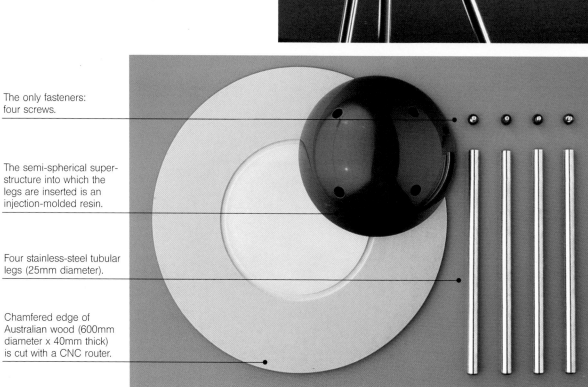

The only fasteners:
four screws.

The semi-spherical super-
structure into which the
legs are inserted is an
injection-molded resin.

Four stainless-steel tubular
legs (25mm diameter).

Chamfered edge of
Australian wood (600mm
diameter x 40mm thick)
is cut with a CNC router.

"4300" table

Designer: Anna Castelli Ferrieri (Italian, b. 1918)
Manufacturer: Kartell S.p.A., Noviglio (MI), Italy
Date of design: 1982

Not a new table, its advanced technology reveals it as having been produced by Kartell, the far-sighted 50-year-old firm which made plastics respectable for domestic use. Composed of only nine pieces (the top, four legs, and four leg cones), the table is easily shipped and assembled. No screws are necessary since all elements are force fitted by the end user.

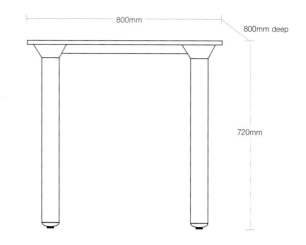

800mm
800mm deep
720mm

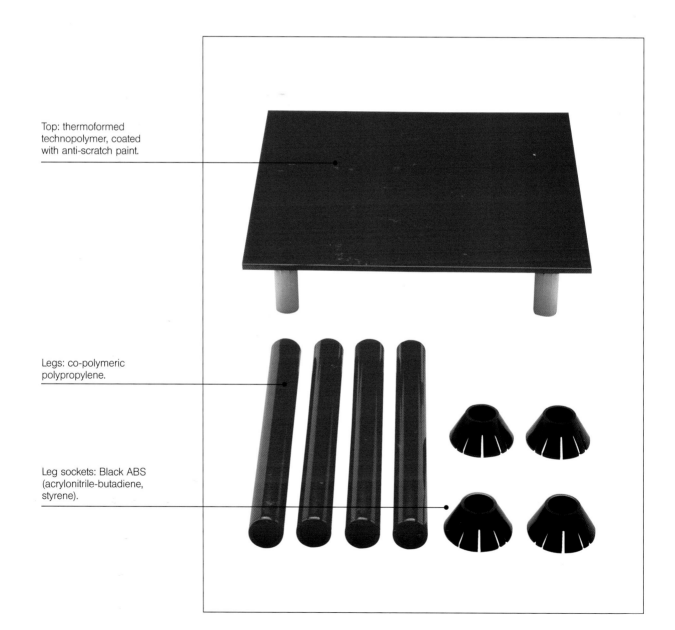

Top: thermoformed technopolymer, coated with anti-scratch paint.

Legs: co-polymeric polypropylene.

Leg sockets: Black ABS (acrylonitrile-butadiene, styrene).

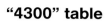

31

"4300" table

Available in white, yellow, green, red, brown, or black.

Underside view of the top.

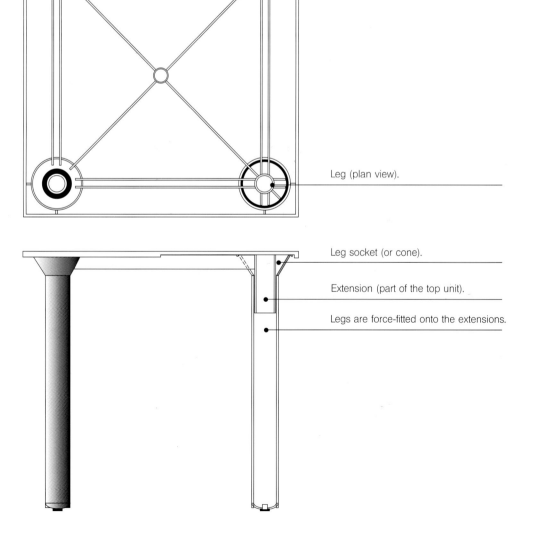

Leg socket (or cone) (plan view).

Leg (plan view).

Leg socket (or cone).

Extension (part of the top unit).

Legs are force-fitted onto the extensions.

"Le misanthrope" console

Designer: Vincent Bécheau (French,
b. 1955) and Marie-Laure Bourgeois
(French, b. 1955)
Manufacturer: the designers
Date of design: 1985

Made primarily of synthetic materials, this
table's main feature, including that of the
other furniture pieces in the same series, is
the use of a particular type of corrugated
polyester sheeting as that for architectural
roofing.

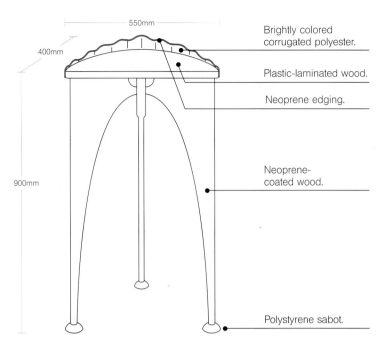

The corrugated polyester top rail is connected
with screws and washers. All other parts are
glued together.

The "Misanthrope" table is part of a system which includes shelving and other
furniture units. A catalogue page is shown below.

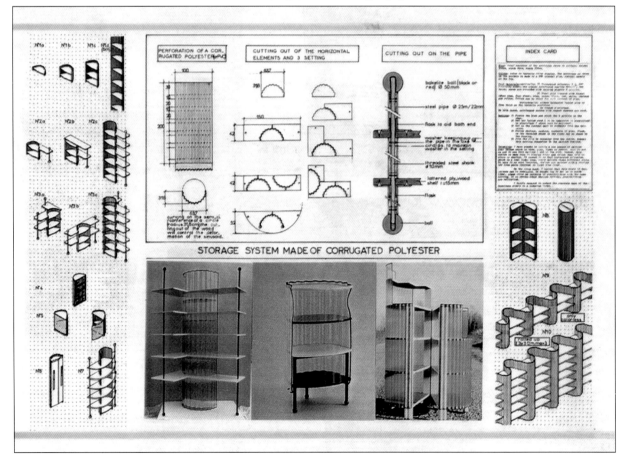

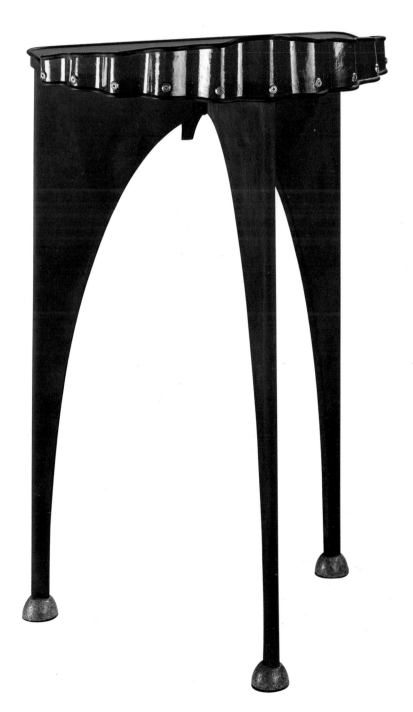

"So" side table

Designer: Andrew Tye (British, b. 1968)
Manufacturer: the designer
Date of design: 1996

The body of this table is composed of flat and bent acrylic sheeting. Since certain plastic materials, such as acrylics, have a shape memory, a heat-bending device is used to set the form of the bottom portion of the body and to retain rigidly vertical and flat planes. To eliminate hard, sharp edges, they are flame flashed.

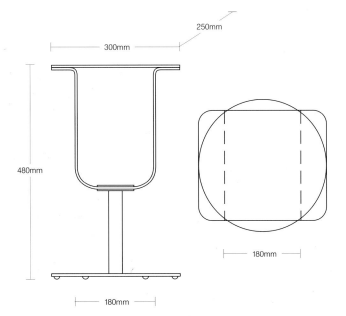

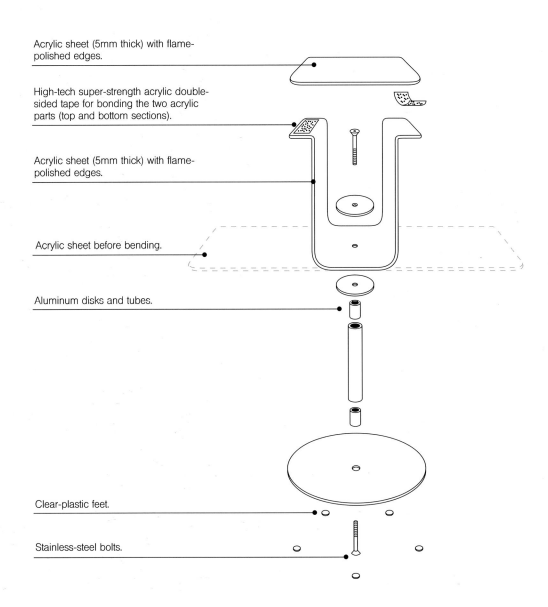

Acrylic sheet (5mm thick) with flame-polished edges.

High-tech super-strength acrylic double-sided tape for bonding the two acrylic parts (top and bottom sections).

Acrylic sheet (5mm thick) with flame-polished edges.

Acrylic sheet before bending.

Aluminum disks and tubes.

Clear-plastic feet.

Stainless-steel bolts.

"A" table

Designer: Maarten van Severen
(Belgian, b. 1956)
Manufacturer: the designer
Date of design: 1992

This sleek, highly engineered table
features the unusual use of what
some might consider an old-fashioned
material, Bakelite, that is glued to the
superstructure. To complete the effect
of the already sleek surfaces, the table
is polished and waxed after being fully
assembled by welding, screwing, and
gluing. Compare this table with the
"Less" table on pages 56–60.

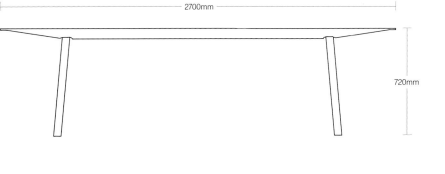

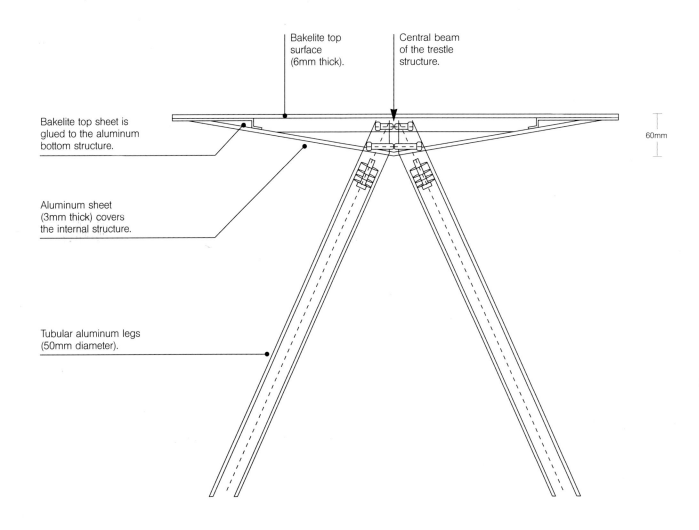

Bakelite top
surface
(6mm thick).

Central beam
of the trestle
structure.

Bakelite top sheet is
glued to the aluminum
bottom structure.

Aluminum sheet
(3mm thick) covers
the internal structure.

Tubular aluminum legs
(50mm diameter).

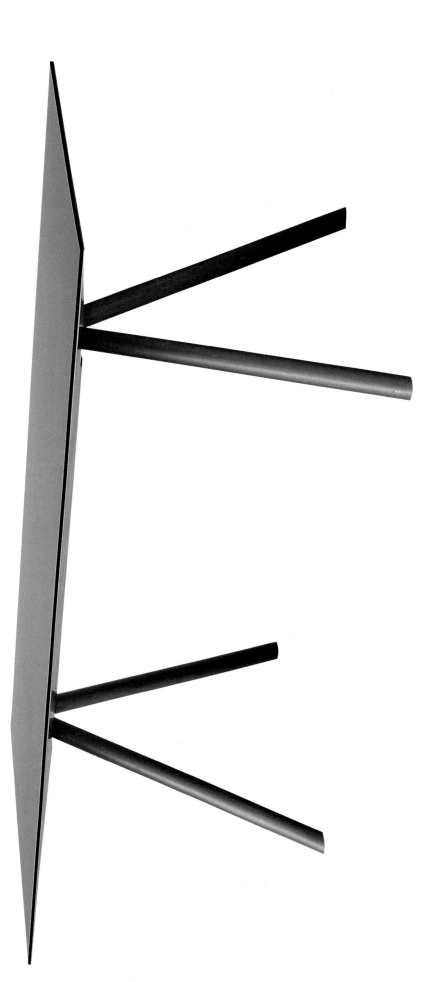

"Triangle" side table

Designer: Hannu Kähönen (Finnish, b. 1948)
Manufacturer: Moform OY, Helsinki, Finland
Date of design: 1986

This collapsible table employs all high-tech, newly developed materials—a surprising departure and non-traditional approach since it was designed and produced in a country known primarily for its use of wood and wood products. The table is part of a suite which includes the "Moform" chair that uses the same materials with the addition of a textile for the arms and seat.

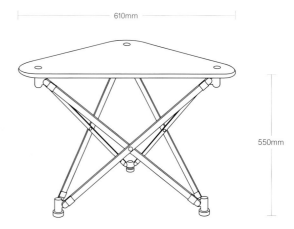

610mm

550mm

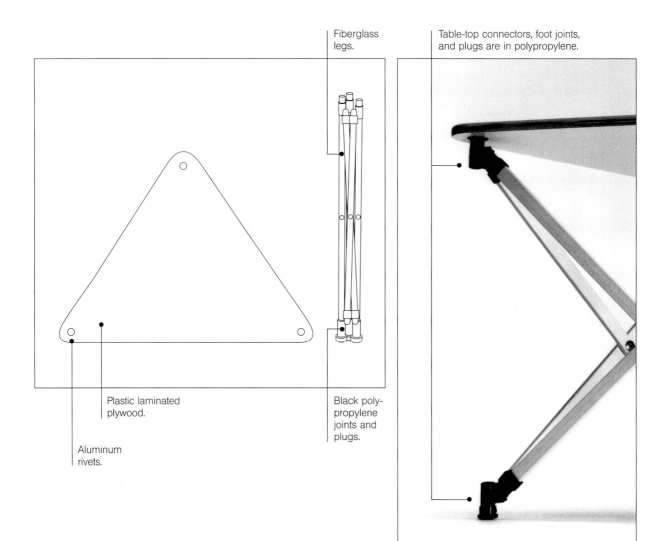

Fiberglass legs.

Table-top connectors, foot joints, and plugs are in polypropylene.

Plastic laminated plywood.

Aluminum rivets.

Black poly-propylene joints and plugs.

"Triangle" side table

The "Triangle" table is part of a suite which includes the "Moform" chair that uses the same materials with the addition of a textile for the arms and seat.

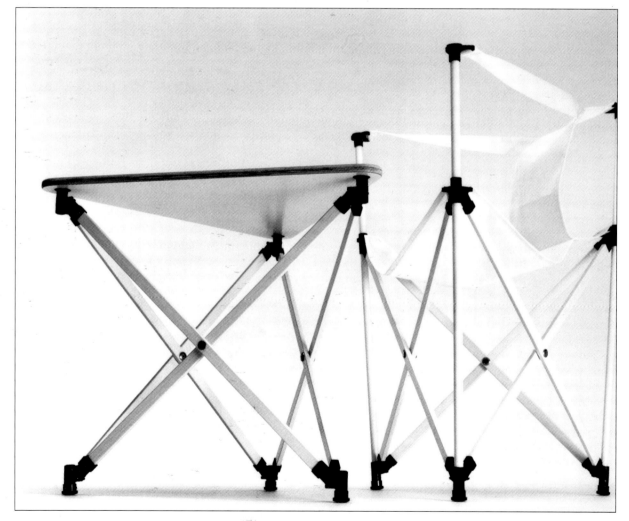

Various Materials

36

"Zébulon" desk

Designer: Jérôme Gauthier (French,
b. 1970)
Manufacturer: the designer
Date of design: 1995

This one-of-a-kind object may appear
peculiar at first view, but, when compared
to narrow-use French furniture of
the 18th century, rationale of the design
may be easier. The eclectic combination
of materials (industrial metal, unfinished
wood, and natural-color leather) is
distinctive in the treatment of the
bellows-pockets.

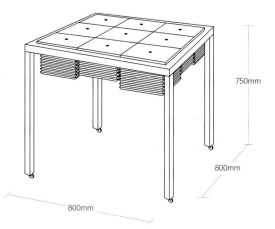

750mm

800mm

800mm

A drawing by the designer
reveals his studies for the
bellows in sheep leather,
including the corner solution
(lower right).

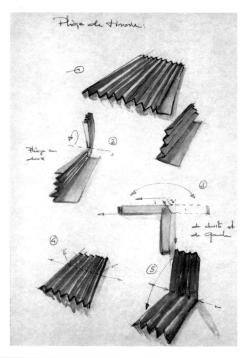

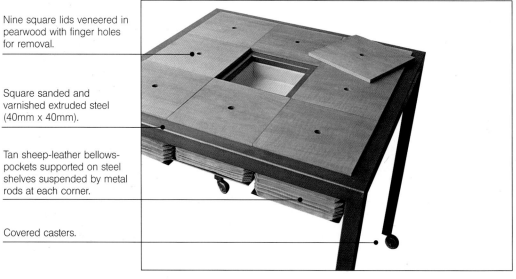

Nine square lids veneered in
pearwood with finger holes
for removal.

Square sanded and
varnished extruded steel
(40mm x 40mm).

Tan sheep-leather bellows-
pockets supported on steel
shelves suspended by metal
rods at each corner.

Covered casters.

Desk-table

Designer: Olivier Leblois (French, b. 1947)
Manufacturer: Quart de Poil', Paris, France
Date of design: 1995

Die cut from the same standard cardboard used to make packing boxes, this
very inexpensive table is sold flat, and
the end user assembles it at home. By
simply using a sharp knife or fine saw, its
height can be changed from high,
as a desk, to low, as a center table.

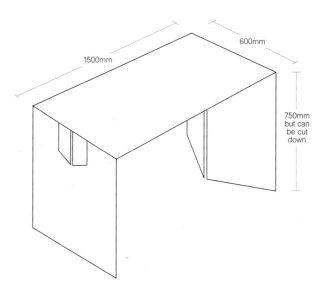

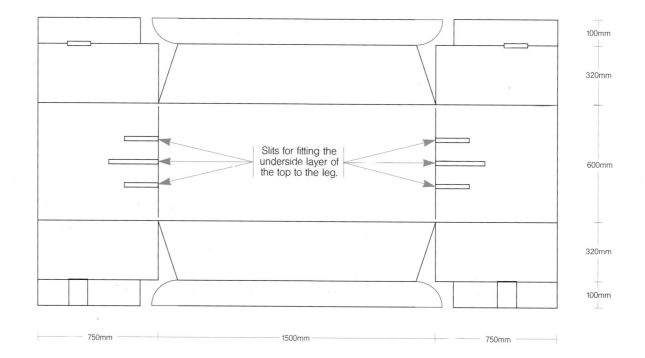

Slits for fitting the
underside layer of
the top to the leg.

100mm
320mm
600mm
320mm
100mm

750mm · 1500mm · 750mm

37

Desk-table

From one piece of corrugated cardboard the table is
built by folding only—no fasteners or glue required.

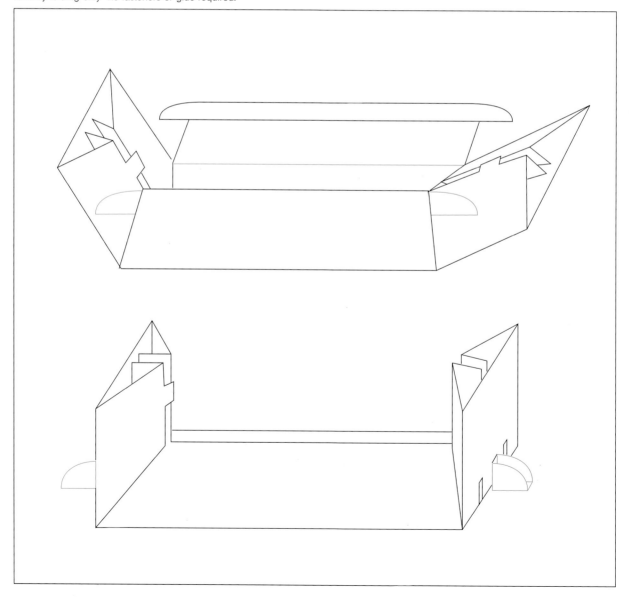

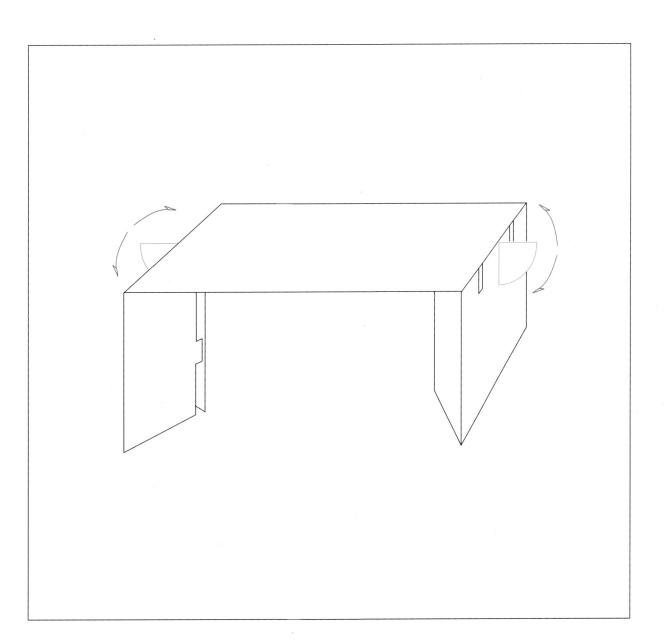

38

"Table cruelle pour jeune fille au pair" table

Designer: Rashdar Coll-Part
(Monégasque, b. 1912)
Manufacturer: the designer
Date of design: 1991

A one-of-a-kind piece, this table is a surreal statement in every aspect. The designer's name is a pseudonym; his date of birth and nationality is probably untrue; and the table itself is a wild flight of fancy. Its title means "a cruel table for two girls." The glass-covered maze simulates a laboratory experiment, and the designer suggests the inclusion of two live mice.

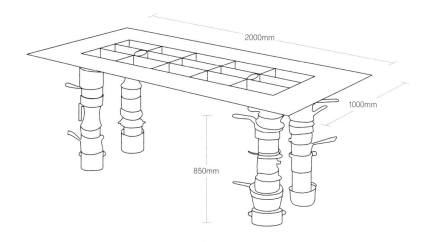

2000mm

1000mm

850mm

Ordinary used pots and pans retaining their original, if tattered, finishes.

The maze is composed of vertically placed sections of aluminum sheeting.

Sécurit (tempered) glass (6mm thick) covers the maze.

Oxidized aluminum top surface (2mm thick).

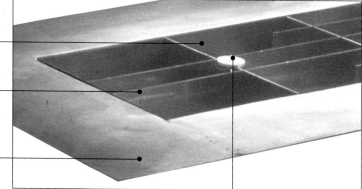

Polyurethane pads separate the glass top from the maze partitions.

"Teppich-Tisch" (rug table)

Designer: Konstantin Grcic (German, b. 1965)
Manufacturer: Authentics, artipresent GmbH, Holzgerlingen, Germany
Date of design: 1993

Produced by a firm known for its products in inexpensive plastics, this table is very odd indeed but possesses an intriguing sense of humor. It is an amalgam of worldwide production elements: rug from India, top from Germany, metalwork from Taiwan, and conception by a designer whose origins are Yugoslavian. The rug table, available in two versions, is purchased by the consumer in three pieces which must be assembled by them.

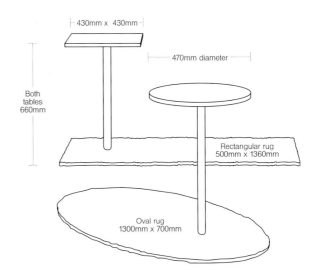

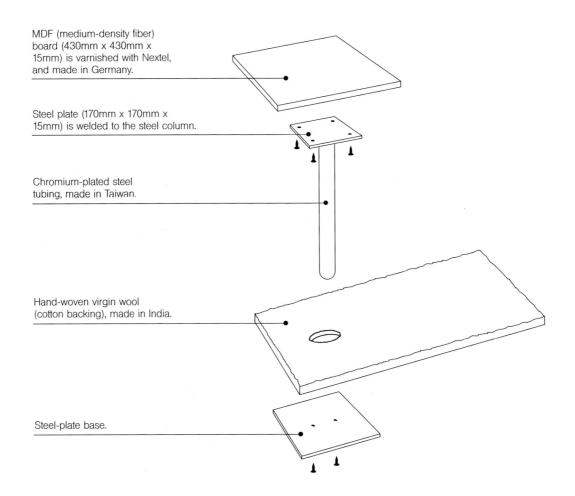

MDF (medium-density fiber) board (430mm x 430mm x 15mm) is varnished with Nextel, and made in Germany.

Steel plate (170mm x 170mm x 15mm) is welded to the steel column.

Chromium-plated steel tubing, made in Taiwan.

Hand-woven virgin wool (cotton backing), made in India.

Steel-plate base.

"Pigmento" center table

Designer: Luciana Martins (Brazilian,
b. 1967) and Gerson de Oliveira
(Brazilian, b. 1970)
Manufacturer: the designers
Date of design: 1995

According to the designers, this table
was conceived as a tribute to materials,
making little other statement, thus the
simple form (the square) and the use
of a raw pigment. They suggest that
the object may only exist for someone
to sit and gaze at it; the intensity of color
is certainly mesmerizing.

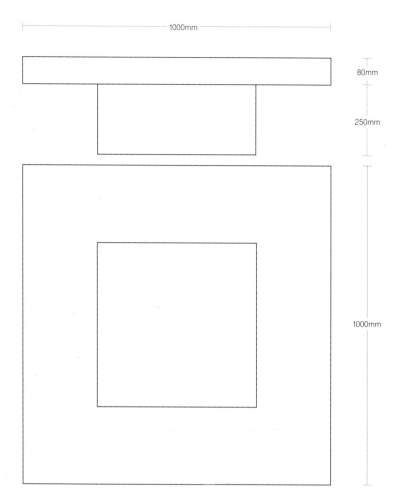

1000mm

80mm

250mm

1000mm

500mm x 500mm

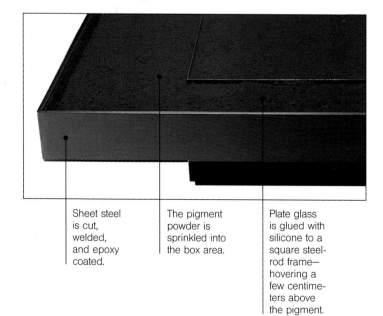

Sheet steel
is cut,
welded,
and epoxy
coated.

The pigment
powder is
sprinkled into
the box area.

Plate glass
is glued with
silicone to a
square steel-
rod frame—
hovering a
few centime-
ters above
the pigment.

40

"Pigmento" center table

The pigment powder, deposited into the box area of
the table, is like that for tinting plastics, dyes, and paints.

Articulation

"Clack" table

Designer: Michele De Lucchi (Italian,
b. 1951)
Manufacturer: Bieffe di Bruno Ferrarese
S.p.A., Caselle di Selvazzano (PD), Italy
Date of design: 1989

This version of the tilt-top table, popularized
in the 18th century, is appropriate for saving
space in small environments. The top folds
downward, and the legs collapse inward,
like an umbrella. Made in metal, it gives the
appearance of wood. There are two sizes of
tops available, named the "Big Clack" and
"Little Clack" tables.

The rectangular hollow metal legs
are attached by the end user to the
folding mechanism at the base of
the short pedestal by means of a
hex screwdriver, provided
with the table.

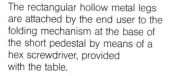

80mm x 80mm or 80 mmx 120mm

Top-locking mechanism.

Folding top.

720mm

25mm

50mm

Folding legs.

41

"Clack" table

Beechwood top
with ingot border.

Tubular steel column
(50mm x 50mm).

Four rectangular hollow-metal
legs (50mm x 25mm x 532mm)
are attached to the central
column mechanism with
a small screwdriver provided
to the end user for assembly.

A drawing by the designer discloses the same leg-folding conception, here for a coat rack.

"S 1080" side table

Designer: Alfredo Walter Häberli
(Argentine, b. 1964) and
Christophe Marchand (Swiss, b. 1965)
Manufacturer: Gebrüder Thonet GmbH,
Frankenberg, Germany
Date of design: 1996

While a stacking chair is quite ordinary
in the history of 20th-century furniture,
a stacking table is unusual. However,
nesting tables have existed for some time.
Available with two slightly different frame
configurations, only one is shown here.
The plastic for the parts alone attests to the
employment of sophisticated technology
in producing this piece: polyamide,
polyacetal, polypropylene, and
thermo-plastic rubber.

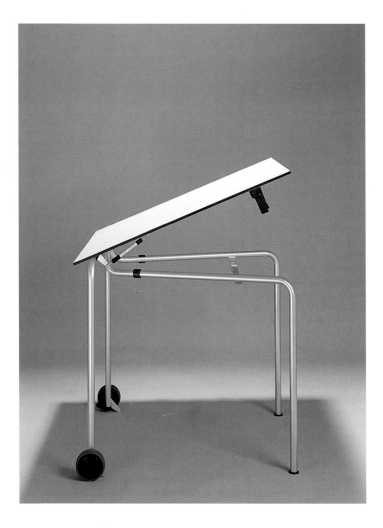

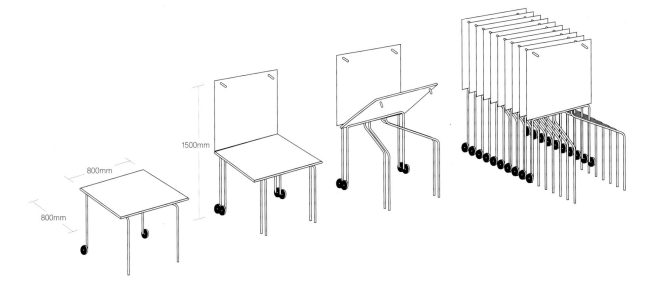

42

"S 1080" side table

The tops are liftable thus exposing the frames which permit the units to be compressed one over the other. Since there is no downward weight as with stacking chairs, an infinite number of tables can be nested.

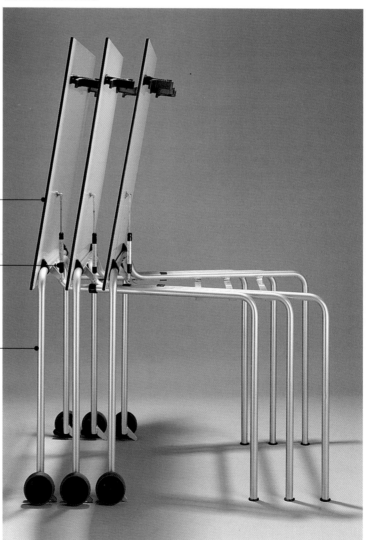

Lid of the table is plastic laminated on the top and on the bottom.

A gas-spring (400N) holds the lid aloft.

High-gloss powder-epoxy coated steel tube (25mm diameter, 2.5mm wall) is bent with a Pulzer type HD35 Matic F machine and soldered.

Assembly is accomplished with ten cylindrical screws and Loctite 454 instant adhesive. Black plastic parts made of polyamide, polyacetal, polypropylene, or thermoplastic rubber.

One of two of Thonet's production facilities in
Frankenberg, Germany, where the table is made.

"Rotterdam" side table

Designer: Alexander Gelman (Russian, b. 1967)
Manufacturer: Nina Sue Nusynowitz, New York, NY, U.S.A.
Date of design: 1997

The top open spaces between the nine folding panels of this metal table can be made narrow in order to eliminate the necessity of a traditional top surface. Shapes, formed by folding, can be any one of a vast number of configurations. The geometry is simpler even than the forms of origami.

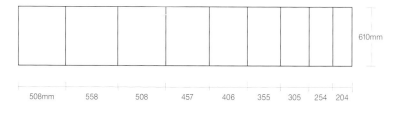

									610mm

508mm	558	508	457	406	355	305	254	204

Flat elevation view

Capable of assuming an almost endless number of shapes and of supporting objects, a separate flat top surface is not needed.

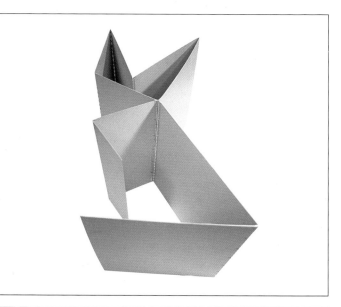

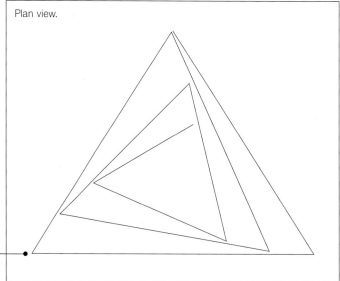

Plan view.

Each section in white-galvanized sheet aluminum (18 gauge) is punched along the sides and fitted with full, vertical Royal hinges (13mm knuckles, 13mm leaves), attached by stainless-steel screws (.08 with round heads) to the edges of the sections.

"Tabula Rasa" table-seat

Designer: Uwe Fischer (German, b. 1958)
and Klaus-Achim Hein, German, b. 1955)
Manufacturer: Vitra AG, Weil am Rhein,
Germany
Date of design: 1987

This structure is a highly practical, though
fantastic, unit that combines seating, table
top, and sideboard. It may be a simple matter
to conjure this concept on the drawing board
or by computer but to have it actually
realized in an edition of 20 is quite another.
Up to a 5000mm length of seating and table
top extends, as if by magic, from the small
cabinet.

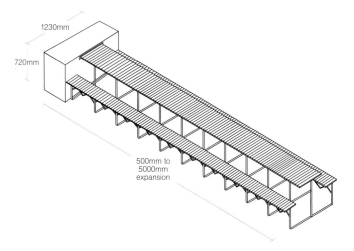

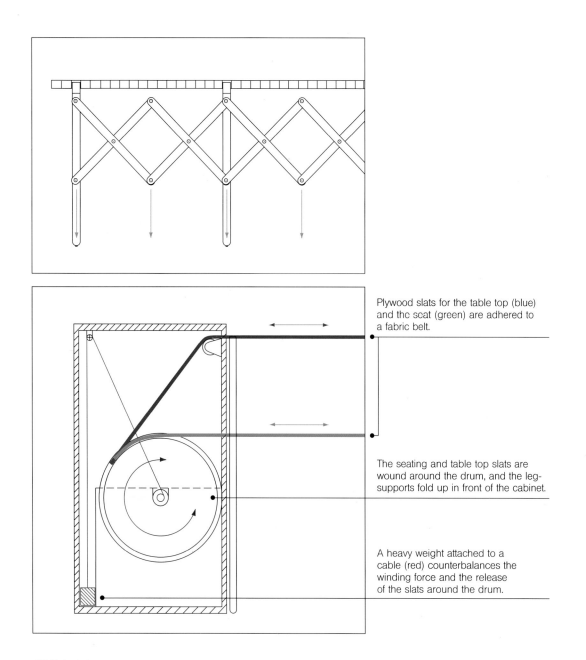

Plywood slats for the table top (blue)
and the seat (green) are adhered to
a fabric belt.

The seating and table top slats are
wound around the drum, and the leg-
supports fold up in front of the cabinet.

A heavy weight attached to a
cable (red) counterbalances the
winding force and the release
of the slats around the drum.

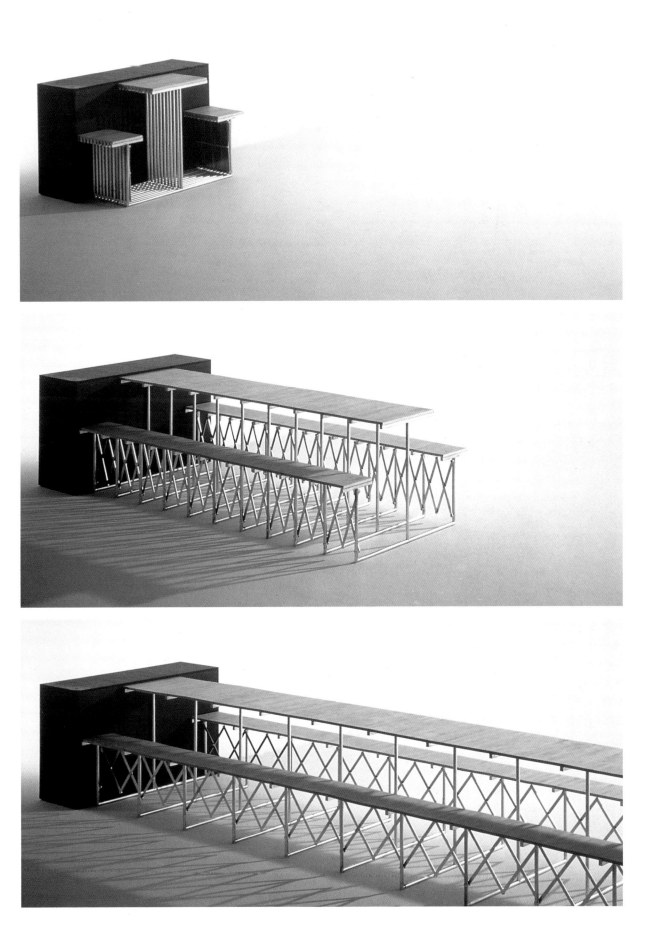

"T Four 4" folding trolley

Designer: Ron Arad (Israeli, b. 1951)
Manufacturer: Driade S.p.A., Fossadello di
Caorso, Italy
Date of design: 1993

A clever folding frame, for easy storage, was
invented to support the plywood tray. This
is a highly refined product by a designer
whose earlier work was much more rough
hewn with obvious, if not brutal, features
revealing handmade construction.

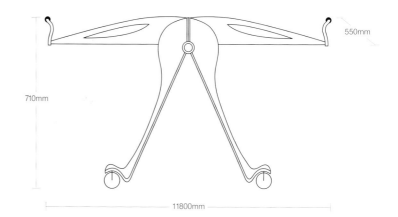

710mm
550mm
11800mm

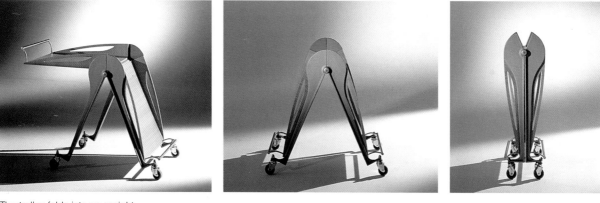

The trolley folds into an upright
position for storage.

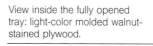

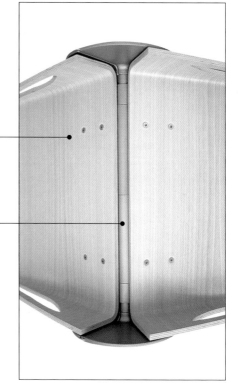

View inside the fully opened
tray: light-color molded walnut-
stained plywood.

Frame in cast aluminum
on casters.

"Last Minute" table

Designer: Hauke Murken (German, b. 1963)
Manufacturer: Nels Holger Moormann,
Aschau im Chiemgau, Germany
Date of design: 1992

In the tradition of using fabric hinges like
those employed by Charles and Ray
Eames in their screen of 1946, the hinges
are the only elements which hold this table
together and make articulation possible.
Easily stowed away, the almost cube-
shaped table can be folded and then
hung on the wall as a space-saving
gesture.

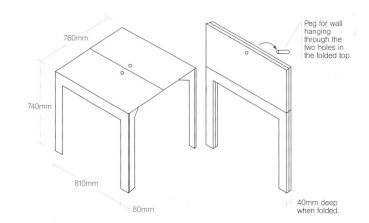

Peg for wall
hanging
through the
two holes in
the folded top.

760mm
740mm
810mm
80mm
40mm deep
when folded.

Partially folded,
completely open,
and hanging stages.

Partially
raised
top.

Hole (36mm diameter) for wall hanging
when the two linen-hinged sections of
the top are folded flat.

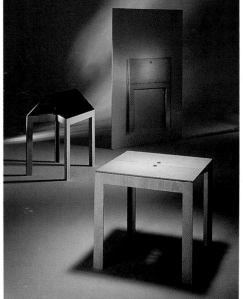

12mm-thick plywood
throughout.

Linen hinge here (at the
center of two opposite aprons)
and at each of the four leg
corners—no other connectors.

Inward-folding apron
(80mm high).

"Scalandrino" table/étagère

Designer: Achille Castiglioni (Italian, b. 1918)
Manufacturer: Zanotta S.p.A., Nova Milanese (MI), Italy
Date of design: 1983

This table can be easily transformed from a flat, horizontal surface into a vertical shelving unit through the use of a releasing-and-locking lever. The kind of tour-de-force object one has come to expect from this venerable designer, this object may be more of an oddity than a practical piece of furniture.

800mm

720mm

1510mm

Configuration can be flat as a table, vertical as a bookcase/shelving unit (above), or angled as a bookcase/ shelving (right).

Natural beechwood shelves with gray-brown or grey-green linoleum inserts.

Silver-painted steel structure.

"Table à bascule"

Designer: Jean-Pierre Caillères (French, b. 1941)
Manufacturer: Papyrus, Paris, France
Date of design: 1985

This two-position table may be used at a dining or desk height or at a center table height. The red spring-buttons at the sides of the weighted base hold the arms in one of two positions.

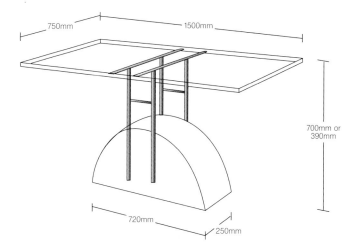

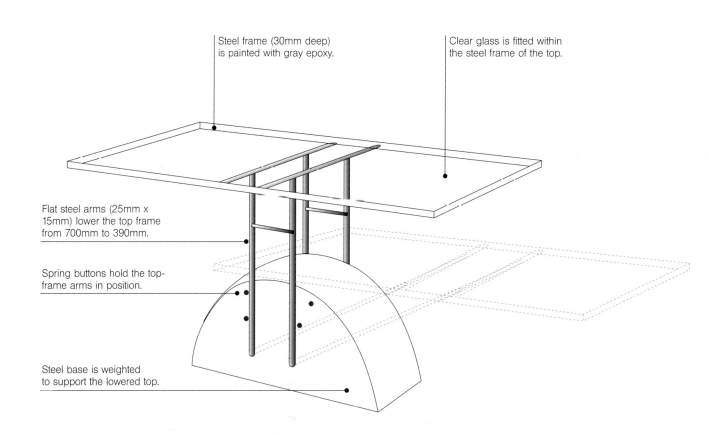

Steel frame (30mm deep) is painted with gray epoxy.

Clear glass is fitted within the steel frame of the top.

Flat steel arms (25mm x 15mm) lower the top frame from 700mm to 390mm.

Spring buttons hold the top-frame arms in position.

Steel base is weighted to support the lowered top.

"Unitisch" system

Designer: Ueli Biesenkamp (German, b. 1941)
Manufacturer: Atelier Alinea, Basel, Switzerland
Date of design: 1995

This system was designed so that any one of a number of possible conditions could be created with varying heights and user-specified top lengths. Configurations include small side tables adjacent to those that tilt for drafting, as well as a desk version (shown here). One top-surface option features a hand-size slit which is cut into the top, making transportation easier.

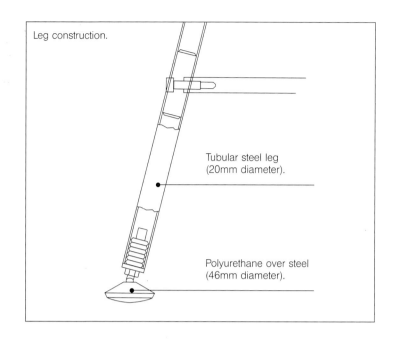

Leg construction.

Tubular steel leg (20mm diameter).

Polyurethane over steel (46mm diameter).

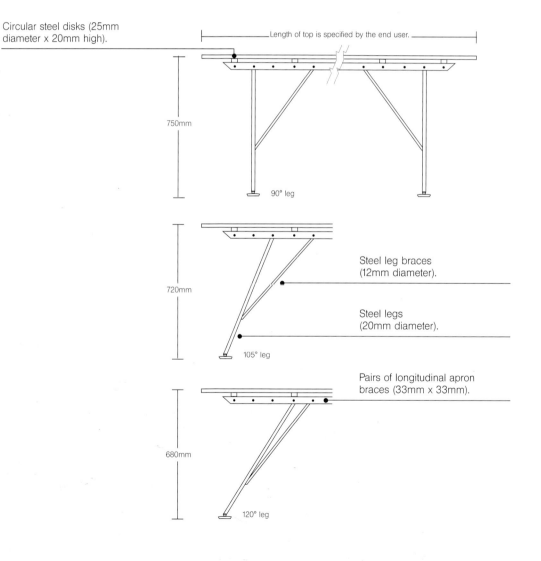

Circular steel disks (25mm diameter x 20mm high).

Length of top is specified by the end user.

750mm

90° leg

720mm

Steel leg braces (12mm diameter).

Steel legs (20mm diameter).

105° leg

Pairs of longitudinal apron braces (33mm x 33mm).

680mm

120° leg

49

"Unitisch" system

Table may be stowed away. The hole in the top
is for hand insertion to facilitate moving.

Top materials and three available designs.

Top surface is available in beechwood, birchwood, or plastic laminate.

"Aluwelle":
Two layers of plywood separated by aluminum struts.

"Multi-Steg":
Two layers of plywood separated by eight-ply wood struts.

"Multiplex":
Single layer of plywood
(10 plies thick).

"Pari" table

Designer: William Sawaya (Lebanese, b. 1948)
Manufacturer: Sawaya & Moroni S.p.A., Milano (MI), Italy
Date of Design: 1986

This table by an experienced, prolific furniture designer and manufacturer of his own work and that of others features a height-altering ability. An easily deployable leg-folding mechanism allows for two heights to accommodate various social functions.

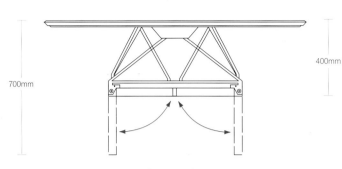

Elevation view.

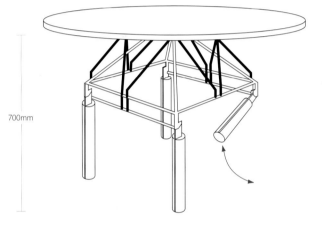

Plan view.

In the high position, the table is appropriate for dining or games.

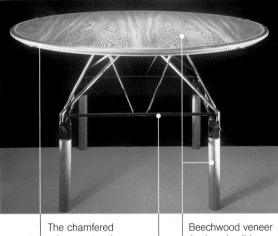

The chamfered edge creates the illusion of an edge thinner than it is.

Beechwood veneer (top) and solid beechwood legs.

Black-painted steel folding mechanism permits two heights.

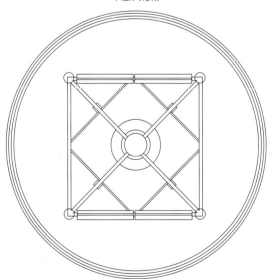

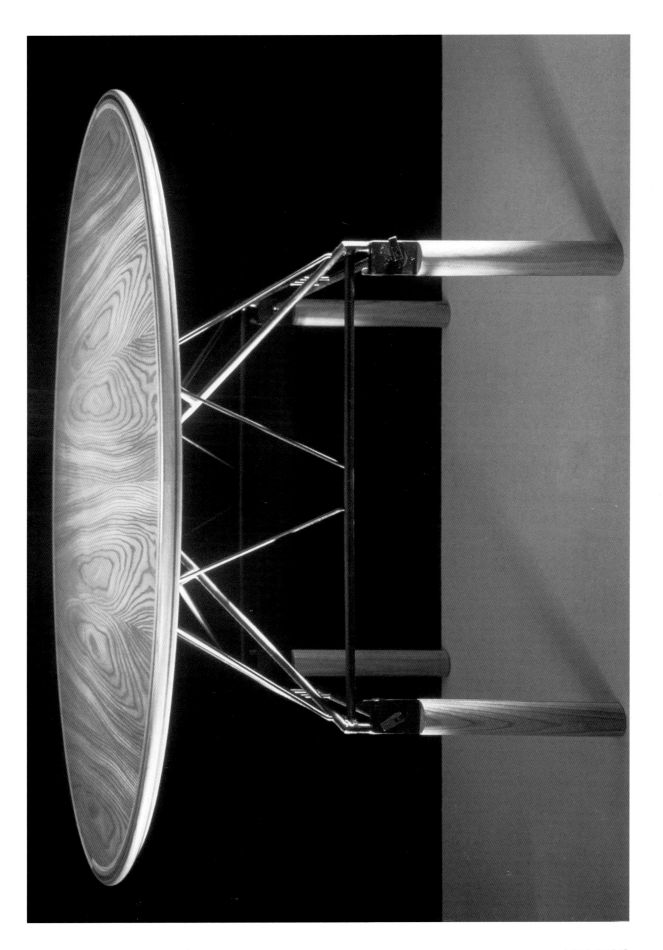

50

When the legs are folded, a center table is created.

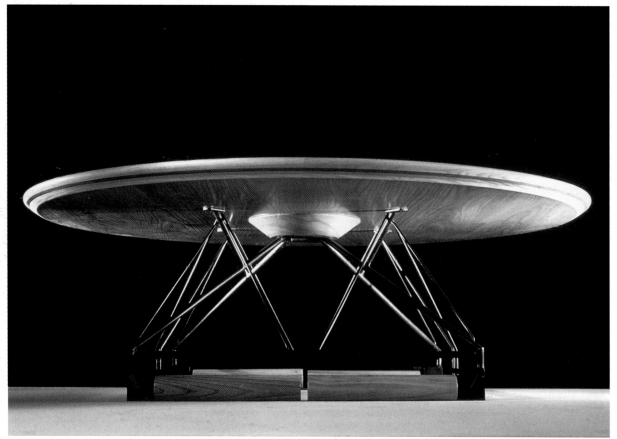

Indices

Designers

Manufacturers

Index

Index

Permissions

Photography, artwork, and drawings (which has been digitally redrawn) were generously provided by the following contributors, preceded by page numbers:

13 Axel Kufus
14–15 Stephan Maria Rother (photog.)
16–17 André Haarscheidt and
  Nicole Zachmann (photog.)
18 Isabelle Millet/Quart de Poil'
20–21 Christain Ghion and Patrick
  Nadeau/Fillioux & Yum (photog.)
22–23 Inredningsform AB
24–25 Carlo Bimbi
26–27 Laura Agnoletto and
  Marzio Rusconi Clerici
26 Cinzia Anguisola (photog.)
27 Carlo Lavatori (photog.)
28 Katsushi Nagumo
30–31 Vitra AG
32–33 Susanne Papake (photog.)
34–36 Nels Holger Moormann
34–36 Tom Vack (photog.)
38–39 David design ab and
  Johan Kalén (photog.)
40–41 Alberto Liévora
42–43 David design ab and
  Johan Kalén (photog.)
44–45 Steel, divisione della Molteni &
  Molteni S.p.a.
46–49 M. Masera (photog.)
50–51 Sergi Devesa and Oscar Devesa
52–53, 55 Pietro Carrieri (photog.)
56–60 Marco Carrieri (photog.)
62 (bottom) Cinzia Anguissola d'Altoé
  (photog.)
62–63 Vincenzo Lauriola
64–65 Philippe Chaix and
  Jean-Paul Morel
66–67 Chérif
68–70 Fiam Italia S.p.A.
72–73 IKEA
74–75 Sylvain Dubuisson
76–77 MAP (Merchants of Australian
  Products)
78 Fernando Campana and
  Huberto Campana
78–79 Andrés Otero (photog.)
80–81 Wolo (photog.)
82–83 Marc Newson and
  Tom Vack (photog.)
86–89 Alberto Meda and Sellitto (photog.)
90–91 Marc Harrison/ANTworks
92–95 Anna Castelli Ferrieri
96 Vincent Bécheau and
  Marie-Laure Bourgeois
97 A. Béguerie (photog.)
98–99 Andrew Tye
100–101 Maarten van Severen
102–104 Moform OY

106–107 Jérôme Gauthier
108 Quart de Poil'
113 Rolan Menegon (photog.)
114–115 Authentics, artipresent GmbH
116–118 Luciana Martins and
  Gerson de Oliveira
120–123 Michele De Lucchi
124–127 Gerbrüder Thonet GmbH
128–129 Alexander Gelman
130–131 Vitra AG
132 (bottom) Cinzia Anguissola d'Altoé
132–133 Driade S.p.A.
134–135 Nels Holger Moormann and
  Tom Vack (photog.)
136–137 Marino Ramazzotti (photog.)
138–139 Jean-Pierre Caillères
140–143 Atelier Alinea
141, 143 Croci & du Fresne (photog.)
144–145 William Sawaya and
  Marco Schillaci (photog.)

Acknowledgements

The Pro-Design series was developed from
an original idea by the late Jean Koefoed.

The following people were very helpful
in the preparation of this book. Its value,
if any, is due to their generous assistance
and also that of the manufacturers' representatives and designers whose work
is discussed here.

Paola Antonelli, The Museum of
  Modern Art, New York
Arlette Barré-Despond
Harriet Bee, The Museum of Modern Art,
  New York
George M. Beylerian, Material Connexion
Dr. Claire Bonney
Judith Brauner, Vitra GmbH
Isabelle Denamur
Olivier Gagnère
Alexander Gelman
Arlene Hirst, *Metropolitan Home*
Ivan Luini
Murray Moss, Moss
Susanne Papke, Vitra GmbH
Stephen Van Dyk, Cooper-Hewitt
  National Design Museum Library

XTTX 83WG

XTTX 83WG